CREOLEDOM

A Study of the Development of Freetown Society

CREOLEDOM

A Study of the Development of Freetown Society

ARTHUR T. PORTER

Professor of History
Fourah Bay College, the University College of Sierra Leone

LONDON
OXFORD UNIVERSITY PRESS
1963

Oxford University Press, Amen House, London E.C.4

GLASGOW NEW YORK TORONTO MELBOURNE WELLINGTON
BOMBAY CALCUTTA MADRAS KARACHI LAHORE DACCA
CAPE TOWN SALISBURY NAIROBI IBADAN ACCRA
KUALA LUMPUR HONG KONG

PRINTED IN GREAT BRITAIN

To my late Mother

who worked hard and sacrificed in order to pay for my secondary education and my undergraduate years at Fourah Bay College.

PREFACE

THE present work is a revision of a dissertation on 'The Development of the Creole Society of Freetown, Sierra Leone: A study in social stratification and the processes of social mobility' which I submitted in 1959 to the Graduate School of Boston University in partial fulfilment of the requirements for the degree of Doctor of Philosophy.

The inspiration behind the subject comes from my formal training in history at Cambridge University in England and my subsequent acquaintance with two social anthropologists with special interests in the problem of social change, namely, Dr Margaret Read, formerly Professor of Education at the Institute of Education, London University, and Dr Kenneth Little, Head of the Department of Social Anthropology at Edinburgh University. Under the auspices of the Social Science Committee of Edinburgh University I was able to spend a year as a research assistant in the Department of Social Anthropology during which time I was able to examine some of the historical records for this study. A grant from the Ford Foundation made it possible for me to undertake formal training in the disciplines of sociology and anthropology at Boston University. With this background I became more convinced of the advantages that can accrue from the collaboration between historians and sociologists for the furtherance of knowledge, both theoretical and practical.

A criticism sometimes levelled at interdisciplinary studies is that each specialist works on the common problem from his own standpoint without achieving the necessary blend which such studies should portray. I trust such criticism cannot be tenable where the collaboration is in the one mind.

The information presented in this study has been gathered in a number of ways, and I have tried wherever possible to give the source of my statements. The area of greatest weakness lies in the absence of the minimum statistical data necessary for an adequate analysis of the community as an on-going social system. The vital statistics on Freetown are difficult and unreliable to use because they are, in the majority of instances, rather crude estimations and, invariably, do not make explicitly clear to what area of the country they refer–whether to the Colony as a whole or to Freetown proper. The fact also that the colony was expanding during the greater part of the nineteenth century makes it even more difficult to compare meaningfully figures from different time periods. While all this connotes caution in the use of such data, it does not spell despair. Fortunately, statistical surveys, however important they may be, do not bring into relief all that is important in the life of a people. And, as Cuber and Kenkel have pointed out in their work on social stratification:

> Historical data, personal observation, and illustrative cases are all empirical and highly useful in this and in many other fields, even though they yield no coefficients of correlation or chi squares.[1]

Franklin Frazier's work on the American Negro is an excellent example of the use that can be made of records of the past to throw light on the contemporary status of the Negro in American society.[2] Similarly, Gilberto Freye's *Casa Grande & Senzala* on social relationships in colonial Brazil is indispensable reading for an understanding of present day race and colour relations in Brazil.[3]

It is in this tradition that I want this study to be viewed; and it is my hope that it will provide the basic guide posts for a fuller understanding of the dynamics of Freetown society and will serve as a necessary background for further studies on the contemporary scene.

It would be tedious to enumerate the names of all who have been of assistance of some kind to me in this work. To all I say thanks. I wish, however, to acknowledge my especial debt to the Sierra Leone Government, the Social Science Committee of Edinburgh University and the Ford Foundation, who made it financially possible for me to avail myself of the opportunities in Europe and America. I am also deeply grateful to Fourah Bay College for granting leave of absence so that I could make use of these opportunities, and for contributing towards the costs of the publication of this book.

[1] Cuber and Kenkel, *Social Stratification* (New York: Appleton-Century-Crofts, 1954), p. 32.

[2] F. Frazier, *The Negro in the United States* (New York: Macmillan, 1949).

[3] Gilberto Freye, *Casa Grande & Senzala*. Trans. by S. Putman as *The Master and the Slaves* (New York: Knopf, 1946).

I wish also to record my appreciation of the encouragement and assistance I have received from Professor William O. Brown, Director of the African Studies Program, Boston University. My thanks also go to the staffs of the Sociology Department and of the African Studies Program of that university, especially to Professors Daniel McCall, Frank Sweetser and Victor Gelineau, who have guided this research, and whose advice and suggestions have saved me from many an error, both of fact and of interpretation.

My thanks are also due to Mr John D. Hargreaves of Aberdeen University for suggesting I revise the manuscript for publication and for providing the introduction to the publishers, in addition to his invaluable corrections of the manuscript; to Mr A. B. C. Thompson, clerk in the History Department at Fourah Bay College, for helping with the typing of the manuscript; and to Mr Christopher Fyfe of London who from his unrivalled knowledge of Sierra Leone records, has provided me with invaluable information for the study here undertaken. Mr Fyfe's own book on the history of Sierra Leone appeared last year while this work was in the press. It deals exhaustively with the history of the Creoles whose patterns of social stratification are here delineated, and might well serve as their apologia as well as their apotheosis. The present work surveys the same period, but from another angle, bringing into clearer relief the institutional outlines of the society and the processes at work in the different stages of its development. I wish also to express my thanks and appreciation to the staff of Oxford University Press for their help, patience and advice from the acceptance of the manuscript to the final printing. Lastly, for reasons too numerous to mention, I owe a great debt to my wife.

Fourah Bay College, A.T.P.
University College of Sierra Leone,
12 October 1962.

CONTENTS

ILLUSTRATIONS

PLATES

MAPS

Introduction

Chapter 1

THE THEORETICAL BACKGROUND

THE curious and distinctive flavour of Freetown which makes it different from other cities and towns in tropical Africa derives mainly from one source, from Creoledom.

The term Creole is used to refer to the descendants of Settlers and Liberated Africans in Sierra Leone and to others who had cultivated their habits and had come to accept their way of living. Their past history is interesting and important and their future rôle in a developing Sierra Leone is no less exciting. But they have their problems and in themselves constitute one of Sierra Leone's immediate problems. Sierra Leone's independence means a common citizenship and this presupposes a sufficient degree of integration of the Creole community with the rest of the country.

If I write of them in the third person, it is not because I do not belong: it is because I want to view them objectively and with detachment, though not without empathy.

This work will attempt to deal with one aspect of Creoledom, namely, the structure of the society and the changes in its shape and span throughout the nineteenth century up to the present time.[1] This knowledge is important for any meaningful understanding of the present social structure and as a basis for any positive efforts at improving human relationships in Sierra Leone.

The theoretical interest of this study centres around Max Weber's conceptualization of social stratification. Karl Marx had earlier focused attention on the differences existing in most human societies by concluding that such differences arose strictly in terms of the economic relations men had with one another. Weber, on the other hand, while acknowledging the

[1] Barber defines space and span as follows: 'Span has to do with the degree of differential evaluation between social class at the top of a stratification system and the class at the bottom. The shape . . . has to do with and results from the proportions of people in a society who are located in its different social classes.' B. Barber, *Social Stratification* (New York: Harcourt, Brace, 1957), p. 87.

importance of the economic variable, has distinguished three basic criteria which stratify a society simultaneously: the possession of economic goods and opportunities, to which he confined the term 'class'; the possession of social honour and prestige, which he called 'status'; and the possession of political power.

Although the distribution of these three criteria are often highly interrelated, Weber maintained that they can be and often are separate and that each in its own way is important in determining the behaviour of individuals, their style of life, and their life chances.[2]

Some social scientists, as for example, Gerhard Lenski, employ the term 'status crystallization' for situations where there is a close correlation among the factors of social stratification, like class, status and power, and the term 'status inconsistency' for situations where families or individuals rank high on some and low on other variables.[3] Weber further argued that in periods of rapid change, there is a tendency for the 'class' component of stratification to be the most crucial determining factor. He wrote:

> When the bases of the acquisition and distribution of goods are relatively stable, stratification by status is favoured. Every technological repercussion and economic transformation threatens stratification by status and pushes the class situation into the foreground. Epochs and countries in which the naked class situation is of predominant significance are regularly the periods of technical and economic transformations. And every slowing down of the shifting of economic stratification leads, in due course, to the growing of status structures and makes for a resuscitation of the important role of social honour.[4]

One of the most general distinctions which can be applied to stratification is that employed by Ralph Linton between 'achieved' and 'ascribed' status, from which was developed the concept of the 'closed' or caste and the 'open' class type of society. In feudal Europe or pre-industrial India, for instance,

[2] M. Weber, *From Max Weber: Essays in Sociology*. Translated by H. H. Gerth and C. W. Mills (New York: Oxford University Press, 1946), p. 47.

[3] G. Lenski, 'Status Crystallization: A Non-Vertical Dimension of Social Status,' *American Sociological Review*, vol. XIX (1954), pp. 405–13.

[4] M. Weber, op. cit., p. 193.

strata lines were firmly drawn and a man stayed in the station of life to which he was born as did his children and grand-children and those before him. Such societies were stratified by 'ascribed' criteria, characteristics with which one is born and over which one has no control, like sex, family lineage, race and so on. Where ascribed criteria are predominant, the rôle and position of an individual in society was largely determined at birth: his occupation, income, religion, associates, education and sometimes even his wife. On the other hand there are societies where these characteristics are in the control of the individual, where his position in the social structure depends very much on his own efforts and ability. Linton defined the terms thus:

> Ascribed status are those which are assigned to individuals without reference to their innate differences or abilities . . . The achieved statuses are, as a minimum, those requiring special qualities, although they are not necessarily limited to these. They are not assigned to individuals from birth but are left open to be filled through competition and individual effort.[5]

A closed or caste society is therefore one composed of strata based upon ascribed criteria, where there is neither individual nor generational mobility from one stratum to another. The open class structure is based on achieved criteria. There is freedom of association between members of different strata, and vertical mobility is possible and probable from the lowest to the highest strata.

Freetown affords an example of a society which, within a relatively short period, has passed from a predominantly closed to a predominantly open system of stratification. It has also, during the same time, experienced periods of varying economic and social transformations and these are reflected in the degree of crystallization in its stratification structure and in the corresponding primacy of the 'class' or 'status' component.

High status crystallization was possible at the outset in Freetown because of the historical beginnings of the Colony. The former Negro slaves from Europe and the New World who were transplanted to the country between 1787 and 1800 were the

[5] Ralph Linton, *The Study of Man* (New York: Appleton-Century-Crofts, 1936), ch. VII, pp. 115ff.

instruments used by the philanthropists and abolitionists in England to form a settlement in Africa itself where all mankind shall be free. An area was made available for their settlement, and their prior contact with western civilization either in England or America, gave them an added advantage in their dealings and relations with the more indigenous Africans. For these reasons, they constituted a privileged group from the outset, though their benefactors did not confine the 'blessings of civilization' to them alone. On the whole, despite a few reverses, these Negro Settlers responded to the favourable treatment meted out by the British administration and other agencies like the missionary societies, and so helped to consolidate their already privileged position by making use of the opportunities for achievement which the situation afforded. Freetown was thus, at this stage, a particularistic society in which achievement was largely determined on the basis of descent.[6]

To these Settlers were added, between 1808 and 1863, Liberated Africans, people who were rescued from slave ships *en route* to the New World. A Liberated African who was desirous of social mobility in the society as it was then structured had to make the Settler groups his focus of reference, and his process of incorporation into this reference group was facilitated by his success in acquiring the other characteristics which reinforced and strengthened the ascriptive descent status, namely, western education and religion, industrial and economic skills, and western political behaviour.

We can distinguish four relatively distinct periods in the social evolution of the Freetown society. The first–the period of the arrival of the 'Black Poor' in 1787 to about 1830–was one of relative stability and homogeneity. There were no other groups to contest or manipulate the westernized township that was emerging, and the ranking order in terms of the Weberian criteria of class, status and power were filled by the New World

[6] Talcott Parsons regards the open and caste types of norms as specific forms of a more generalized value typology which he has called 'universalistic' and 'particularistic'. The universalistic type of institutional norm prescribes that all men be treated according to the same standards of evaluation. And the particularistic type prescribes the division of men into different categories on the basis of inherited, racial, sexual, family, or community characteristics and their differential evaluation accordingly. Cf. Talcott Parsons, *Essays in Sociological Theory*, rev. edn. (Glencoe, Ill.: Free Press, 1954), ch. 2, 4 and 19. Also, *The Social System* (Glencoe, Ill.: Free Press, 1951), pp. 61–3.

Settlers. It was a period of 'status crystallization'. The next period–1830 to 1870–was one of rapid change during which the colony made significant strides in the economic and political fields. It was a time when individuals from the body of Liberated Africans were gaining recognition by virtue of their success in trade and business. It was thus a period of status inconsistency as already defined when many families and individuals ranked high on the economic variable but low in status or political power. It was a period when the class component was most crucial for mobility, when Settlers and Liberated Africans alike gained or lost in the stratification hierarchy in proportion to their possession of economic goods and opportunities. By the 1870s the Liberated Africans had merged in large enough number with the old westernized Settlers to form the Creole group. It was also a period of stability and a second period of status crystallization with wealth, status and power now in the hands of the upwardly mobile Liberated Africans and those Settlers who had retained their social position. This lasted until about the eve of the Second World War when the society began to experience another period of economic and technological development with accompanying social changes which the war itself and its aftermath have accelerated.

These periods which saw contact between Settlers and Liberated Africans and later a fusion of the two groups to form the Creole community, have also witnessed contact between the small westernized society of Freetown and the indigenous inhabitants of the rest of the country; and it is to be hoped that the succeeding, if not the present, period will see the complete fusion of the two groups in the country. There are in fact a number of similarities between the two processes of contact and change. There were, for example, important changes in the educational system–in the one instance, the provision of schools for the Liberated Africans; in the other, the establishment of western-type schools in the provinces. Education was thus a crucial instrument providing, first the Liberated Africans and then the tribal Africans, with the knowledge and skills necessary for movement into new and more highly valued rôles than those occupied by their parents. Further, changes occurred and are occurring in the political and judicial spheres by legal enactments and extensions of the franchise which created conditions conducive to an increase in equality and social mobility.

There were also significant differences between these two processes of change which may account for the rate and degree of acculturation that was possible under the respective processes. For one thing, the Liberated Africans were introduced into the society as apprentices (i.e. people to be taught a trade or skill) with the unequivocal desire on the part of the two dominant agencies, the British Government and the missionary societies, that the Liberated African should accept the western culture, a variant of which was practised by the Settlers. The fact also, that the Liberated Africans faced Settler culture as individuals and isolates rendered the task of acculturation easier to accomplish. In the Creole/tribal contact, this desire on the part of the dominant agencies was absent. No attempt was made to incorporate tribal immigrants into the Creole community; instead their cultures were respected and allowed to survive.

Notwithstanding these differences, there are other developments taking place which are influencing and modifying tribal cultures and accelerating the movement of people from one tribal area to another. All these will mean greater fusion and the gradual disappearance of the ethnic factor as a criterion of social stratification.

It should, however, be borne in mind throughout this work, that these time divisions are useful primarily as a matter of expository convenience, and are not intended to convey the impression that each begins and ends a definite process of change.

Changing social relationships, increasing heterogeneity and mobility of populations, citification of formerly rural and tribal communities all point to a movement of Freetown society from a particularistic to a universalistic orientated set of norms.

It is, no doubt, a reasonable expectation that a study of this sort should result in some anticipation as to the future of the Freetown status-reward-power system. It should be remembered, however, that a stratification system is an integral part of a total social system, and therefore is vitally affected by what takes place in the other interdependent areas. Changes in technology, in education, in economic and political structures, and in the predominant ideologies, all affect in varying degrees social relationships and the social stratification system. The relation and interaction of all these varied factors in any process of social change is not something fixed or given. It has to be found in each specific case. Indeed, there is no more certain source for sociological generalizations than historical particularities. In no field is Kant's assertion that history without sociology is blind, and sociology without history is empty, truer than in the study and analysis of class structure. Notwithstanding all this, it seems safe to say that there will not be a return to the caste-like type of society with predominant ascriptive criteria which characterized nineteenth-century Freetown. It is plausible to argue that within a generation there will have evolved a Sierra Leone concept to take the place of the Creole/tribal compartmentalization.

Chapter 2

CREOLEDOM

SIERRA LEONE, of which Freetown is the capital, is situated between 6° 55′ and 10° of North Latitude and 10° 16′ and 13° 18′ of West Longitude on the West Coast of Africa. It covers an area of about 27,925 square miles and, in 1959, had an estimated population of about two and a half million. It was divided into the Colony, which consisted roughly of the peninsula, and the Protectorate. The Colony was that portion which the British Crown had acquired either by cession, annexation or treaty from 1807, and the Protectorate is the large area inland which came under British protection in 1896. Freetown itself is situated at the northern end of the peninsula, at the foot of steep hills, about four miles up the River Sierra Leone. It possesses one of the best natural harbours in West Africa, and was, during the Second World War, a convoy station for ships from Africa making the Atlantic crossing to Europe and the New World. The peninsula was chosen for the settlement in 1787 on the suggestion of Mr Henry Smeathman, who had visited these parts, that it was the most advantageous place for the experiment.[1]

The purpose of the settlement was to secure a home on the continent of Africa for natives of Africa and their descendants who for one reason or another, primarily because of slavery and the slave trade, had left their native shores and were perforce living abroad, as well as for those Africans of what one might call the 'diaspora'.[2]

During this period various groups of people were sent to Sierra Leone, of which four are of major significance for the subsequent development of the settlement. Of these the first was the group of about four hundred 'Black Poor' who were living in and around London, some sixty nondescript white

[1] R. R. Kuczynski, *Demographic Survey of the British Colonial Empire* (London: Oxford University Press, 1948), vol. 1, p. 41.

[2] Used here to refer to those of the African race scattered throughout the world, analogous to the Jews scattered throughout the world after the Exile.

women and a few white men. They arrived in the colony in 1787. In 1791 the Directors of the Sierra Leone Company decided to send to the country Europeans as colonists as well as for the administration of the colony. In that year, according to the Board of Directors' Report, 'one hundred and nineteen white persons' sailed for Sierra Leone. Though these white Settlers did not play any conspicuous part in the subsequent development of the country, yet this decision of the Directors is important as evidence of their intention to accept colonists from all races.

The second significant group was the eleven hundred Negroes from Nova Scotia, Canada, who arrived in Freetown in 1792. These were former American slaves who had supported Britain in the American War of Independence and had been settled as free men or servants of Loyalists in the maritime provinces of Canada. The third group was the Maroons who arrived in 1800. These were Negroes who had revolted against their British masters in the West Indian island of Jamaica, and who, after an offer of equitable peace terms, were tricked into leaving their strongholds and were then captured and removed to Nova Scotia.

Most of the Negro Settlers, with perhaps the exception of the Maroons, had lost their African cultural heritage and had developed new habits to meet the complex situations in the western world. They had evolved a *lingua franca* composed predominantly of English words, and many answered to western names. They thus constituted a small but significant class of black settlers with values and patterns of behaviour different from those of the surrounding tribal Africans.

After the passing of the Slave Trade Act in 1807, a court of adjudicature, the Court of Vice-Admiralty, was established in Freetown for the trial of slave ships and the release of their human cargo. Thus for the next fifty years, a vast number of newcomers were added to the population of the colony. Unlike the earlier Settlers, this fourth group of people were tribal Africans on their way to slavery in the New World. According to Koelle's *Polyglotta Africana*, there were many from as far north as Senegal and as far south as Angola, though Ibo and Yoruba from Nigeria predominated. They represented about as heterogeneous an assemblage, in language, custom and belief as can be imagined.

Freetown became a cultural melting pot. Faced with the western cultural patterns as interpreted by the New World Settlers (i.e. the Nova Scotians predominantly), which patterns were reinforced by the patronage and favour of the European administration and other ancillary agencies like the missionary societies, the Liberated Africans, as this fourth group of immigrants came to be known, began to copy these patterns which soon became the high prestige culture for all groups in the territory.

Around the 1820s, Freetown society was stratified hierarchically into four levels made up of the indigenous inhabitants of the area, the newly arrived Liberated Africans, the Settlers and the English official class (who, as the Administration, were always exemplars of prestige values) in an ascending order of superordination. The structure then exhibited some features of a caste-like or closed society where status was based on ascribed rather than achieved criteria. By the mid-century, a number of Liberated Africans had succeeded in adapting and assimilating the culture of the New World Settler, while, at the same time, influencing settler ways to some extent.

A small minority of Liberated Africans from Yoruba land in Nigeria, however, were able to reassemble at Freetown where they succeeded in maintaining some cohesion and identity by preserving the Yoruba language and embracing the Moslem religion.[3]

Though these factors distinguished them from the rest of the Liberated Africans, yet they were never identified with the indigenous populations of the Freetown area. In fact throughout the nineteenth century they were grouped with others from Yoruba land, being designated generically as 'Akoos' or 'Akus'.[4] However, while their Christian brothers became increasingly removed from traits specifically Yoruba, they clung more tenaciously to their Yoruba folkways, and by the early twentieth century the term 'Aku' had taken on a narrower meaning as referring exclusively to the Creole Moslem groups. Until about

[3] Some were Moslems even before arrival, e.g. 'Three of the discontented Akoos whose names are in the margin (Ogubah, Odhdoo, Soko) came to this office this morning voluntary and gave themselves up. They state that they were of the Mahommedan Faith in their own Country and never had received any Interuption since they were brought to the Colony.' *Sierra Leone Archives*, Liberated African Letter Book 1830–1, pp. 93–4.

[4] Koelle, *Polyglotta Africana* (London, 1854), p. 5.

the eve of the Second World War, they were a community who did not share or contest a share in the status-reward-power system of Freetown. By the mid-century, a number of Liberated Africans had succeeded in adopting and, to some extent, modifying Settler culture and folkways. They were able to do this partly because of the efforts of their benefactors and also by their own efforts. They were not prepared to accept with resignation that station of life in which it had pleased God to call them, but many ventured afield in search of markets and it was primarily through trade that the Liberated Africans began to enter and to participate on a comparatively equal footing in the society the Settlers had created. They could not be guilty, as many now accuse them, of possessing a pensioner mentality which was prepared to have things done for them. The Liberated Africans saw the advantages and seized them. In time the people with wealth began to assume leadership in the various spheres of life and to validate their newly acquired position by inter-marrying with the old status groups and by displaying other forms of social success.

The period after 1870 was perhaps the high water mark of Creole society, when the descendants of new and old world immigrants set the pace in all fields not only for the example of Sierra Leone but for all West Africa. It is true that not all of the Liberated Africans achieved success, and that there was a sizeable proportion of downward social mobility among both Settlers and recaptives. Nevertheless, a number of individuals and families achieved a high ranking in terms of the significant western criteria of stratification, and their culture became a most important formative influence in the development of Sierra Leone.

This dominant position of the Creoles in almost all spheres of life in Sierra Leone went practically unchallenged until about the period of the First World War. The policy of Governor Cardew towards the Creoles, the Hut Tax War consequent on the Declaration of the Protectorate in 1896, competition from Syrian traders and European retail firms, the opening up of the Protectorate by education and commerce, all contributed to the loss of the near-monopoly which the Creoles had enjoyed.

But in the nineteenth century, it was this group of Creoles who held the centre of the stage and whose distinct brand of culture has given the peculiar stamp and colour to Sierra Leone. Many of them migrated to other lands and contributed out of all proportion to their numbers to the development of these territories. True, in this they neglected their own hinterland which militated against an early evolution of a consciousness of common identity between the two parts–Colony and Protectorate–of Sierra Leone. In this they may also have disappointed their benefactors who had hoped that, like leaven, they would influence their more immediate surroundings first. It was not, however, that the Creoles were unmindful of the rest of Africa. It was rather that they preferred to show it in their own way by going to Nigeria, to Ghana and other parts: As Professor Macmillan wrote in 1940:

> As far afield as the Belgian Congo in pre-1914 days, 'Sierra Leoneans' *videlicet* Creoles, were in actual demand as clerks and as artisans and generally in a variety of positions of minor responsibility for which uneducated 'natives' were unsuitable. There still are small but distinctive Creole settlements of such men, 'holding their heads high', in many towns all along the coast. No other section of African society has produced so many individuals who have proved the latent possibilities of Africans.[5]

Sierra Leone has pioneered in many fields, largely because of the rôle of the Creoles and their efforts and ability to enhance their already favourable position. Whether we think of education, or of newspapers or of African representation in the political order, or of entry into the professions, Sierra Leone witnessed the earliest and largest advances. Fourah Bay College, an institution of higher education, was founded in 1827, a boys' secondary school in 1845, and a girls' in 1849. A newspaper was started in 1801 and the first newspaper published by an African was established in 1855. African political representation in the legislature was secured as early as 1863. John Thorpe, the first Sierra Leonean, a Maroon, was called to the English Bar in 1850 and in 1872, Samuel Lewis, the first African to be knighted by a British sovereign, entered the legal profession.

They had developed a sense of group solidarity and class consciousness and this unifying force meant that there was no unnecessary dissipation of potential, and that all worked for the

[5] Meek, Macmillan and Hussey, *Europe and West Africa* (London: Oxford University Press, 1940), p. 75.

development of the society. Their compactness and concentration, mostly in Freetown, made them also more increasingly conscious of their group interests.

There were also, within the boundaries of Sierra Leone, other ethnic or tribal groups. There were about fourteen of these, of whom the Mende in the south-eastern part and the Temne in the north-western are the largest.[6] In addition there are a small number of other racial groups in the country, predominantly Europeans, mostly from Britain, and Asians, largely from the Indian sub-continent and Syria and Lebanon.

There is not, and never was in the nineteenth century, a settler problem in the sense of Europeans living in the country, with a stake in the future of the country and an inclination to share, or contest a share in the same social system. The Asians also do not compete for status, yet they have in the past, particularly the Lebanese and Syrians, been regarded as the sources of some of the decline in the participation of the African in the commerce of his country. As Alldridge noted in 1910:

> The Syrian trader has annexed the West Coast; he has come and come to stay. . . . He is more than a clever man of business; his tact is wonderful, amounting to genius. . . . Content with the 'nimble ninepence' . . . the Syrian saves where the Sierra Leonean squanders. . . . How under the present circumstances, with the importing retailing houses on the one hand and the Syrian gleaners on the other, they are to exist, is with them one of the most serious problems of the day.[7]

Relationships between the various racial groups have involved profound social changes from a situation where the Europeans were at the top of the stratification scale, to the intervening accommodation when Africans with sufficient western criteria were accepted in the higher order of the hierarchy, to the other extreme which is now unfurling with the elevation of Africans into the positions of authority and the whites into dependent if not supplicant and subordinate rôles. Relations between Creoles and tribal Africans have undergone similar profound changes.

[6] e.g. *Atlas of Sierra Leone* (Surveys and Lands Department, Freetown, 1953), p. 9.
[7] T. J. Alldridge, *A Transformed Colony* (London: Seeley, 1910), p. 67.

It is with this background of Freetown as the arena of interaction that we shall examine the changes in the social stratification system. In Part One we shall attempt to trace the evolution of Creole community on a time perspective, and in Part Two we shall deal more analytically with the criteria of stratification.

Part One
HISTORICAL DEVELOPMENT

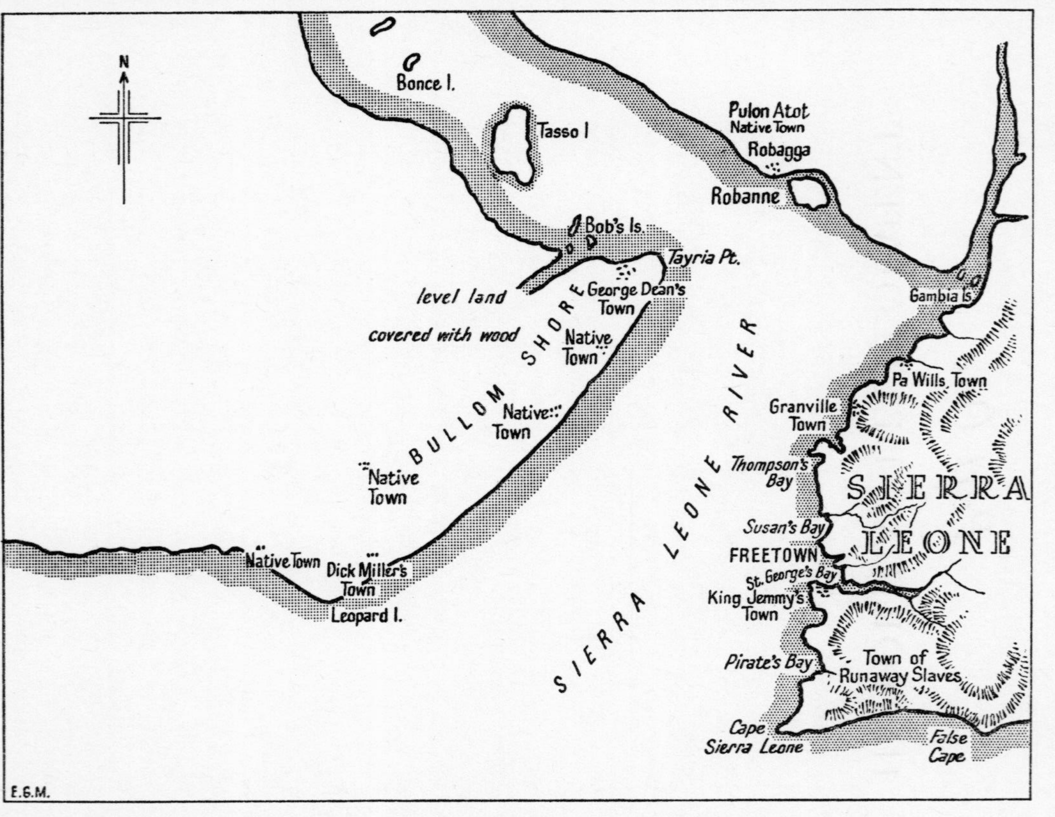

View of the New Settlement in the River at Sierra Leone

Chapter 3

FREETOWN, A BLACK SETTLER COLONY, 1787–1807

THE period from 1787 to 1807–from the arrival of the first Settlers to the end of Company rule in Freetown–saw the beginning of a new experiment in Afro-European relationships. Instead of the old 'middle passage' traffic when Negroes were taken from Africa and sold into slavery in the markets of Europe and the New World, the new 'middle passage' traffic of these years consisted in Negroes making the return journey from Europe and the New World, not for purposes of slavery, but that they might have the opportunity of living their lives as free men on their own native continent. This was to be an answer of humanitarians and liberals to the question of slavery; it was also intended to be one way of introducing industry and western civilization to Africa. While there is now no doubt that the change in economic theory from mercantilism to *laissez faire* affected men's attitude to slavery, yet it would be a prostitution of history not to acknowledge the contribution of the humanitarians and men of ideas to the success of the abolitionist movement.

During these years, groups of Negroes, from Britain, Canada and Jamaica, with a sprinkling of white colonists from England, arrived in Sierra Leone, and set up a way of life which has had tremendous impact and influence on the subsequent development of the territory. In this chapter, we shall consider in turn these several settler invasions and their contribution to the emerging social structure of the colony.

Unlike other settler colonies, Freetown started as a black settler colony. It was conceived as a home in Africa for Negroes whose ancestors had been forcibly transported to Europe and the New World for one reason or another, primarily as slaves to work in the plantations, cotton fields and 'big houses' of their masters.

The first settlers to arrive in the colony were the 'Black Poor' from England. Many of these were Negroes from in and around London who had no employment and who were adding to the social problem of beggars in the city. A good number were former slaves of West Indian plantation owners who had escaped from their masters in consequence of Lord Mansfield's decision in 1772 in the case of the slave, James Somerset, that slavery was not 'allowed or approved by the law of England'. In addition, many of the Negroes were former American slaves. During the American War of Independence, many had entered on board the British ships-of-war or repaired to the British standard. At the peace of 1783, some of them, as well as some of the white loyalists, were conveyed to the Bahamas, some to Nova Scotia, and others to Great Britain.[1]

Partly because they lacked the necessary skills and owing also to the post-war slump, these former slaves found it difficult to obtain employment in England. It is not surprising, therefore, that they soon joined the band of the destitute and the vicious who were creating a social problem in London.

In 1786 the 'humanity of some gentlemen was excited towards the distressed blacks' and a Committee was formed known as 'the Committee for the Black Poor', under the chairmanship of Jonas Hanway, to consider ways and means to alleviate their suffering. The Committee accepted the advice of one Mr Henry Smeathman who had travelled to those parts, that it would be best to repatriate the Negroes to Africa, and recommended Sierra Leone as the most advantageous place for the experiment.[2] The British Government agreed to provide the transports and some of the financial assistance, and a handbill was put out in the name of the Committee inviting those who so desired to accept free passage to Sierra Leone.[3]

It seems that about 500 or 510 passengers–about 440 male and female black and about sixty or seventy male and female white–embarked in Portsmouth, that fifty or more died, twenty-four were discharged, and twenty-three ran away, and that finally 411 (black and white) sailed from Plymouth, of whom

[1] C. B. Wadstrom, *An Essay on Colonization*, London, 1794, vol. II, pp. 227–8.

[2] Henry Smeathman, *Plan of a Settlement to be made near Sierra Leone, on the Grain Coast of Africa: intended more particularly for the service and happy establishment of Blacks and People of colour to be shipped as freemen under the direction of the Committee for Relieving the Black Poor, and under the protection of the British Government*, pp. 16–17. Quoted in Kuczynski, op. cit., p. 41.

[3] Cf. Appendix for *Provisions of the Handbill*.

thirty-four died at sea and 377 arrived in Sierra Leone on 9 May 1787 and disembarked on the 15th.[4]

As regards the Negro passengers, Granville Sharp states that they were 'chiefly Seamen, that had served in the Royal Navy, last War, or as Rangers with the Army in the American Woods'.[5] Later reports indicate that they were all men who had been discharged from the army and navy after the American War.[6] Recent writers say that they were mainly or exclusively Negro slaves brought by their masters to England.[7] It seems more likely, however, that those who had sailed the seas or displayed valour and the adventurous spirit in other contexts would be more readily disposed to make the journey, though there is some evidence that a number of domestic servants in England agreed to join the venture out of excitement at the thought of returning to Africa.[8]

The earliest information about the white women comes from Mrs Anna Maria Falconbridge's account. She wrote that the 'women were mostly of that description of persons who walk the streets of London, and support themselves by the earnings of prostitution'.[9] It is difficult to believe that the British Government and the ardent Christian abolitionists could have been capable of this. The idea of sending unmarried women to a new settlement was not new or heinous in itself, for Wadstrom makes reference in his work to a similar procedure when Van Riebeck began the settlement at the Cape of Good Hope in 1652. Girls from an orphan house in Holland were sent out and were provided with small dowries by the Dutch East India Company on their marriage. It may be that the British Government and the philanthropists were aware of the order to send out unmarried girls, but were not responsible for the choice. An alternative explanation could be that this action was in keeping with the sentiments of the time when undesirable characters

[4] Kuczynski, op. cit., vol. 1, p. 43. This is the most authoritative work on the composition and early history of the various immigrant groups into Sierra Leone at this period.

[5] Wadstrom, op. cit., p. 260.

[6] Great Britain, *Parliamentary Papers*, vol. XI (Report on the West Coast of Africa, 1842), Part II, p. 246.

[7] F. L. Evans, 'An Early Constitution of Sierra Leone', *Sierra Leone Studies* No. XVIII (November 1932), pp. 26–77.

[8] The list of headmen they chose for the journey included five who had served on naval ships and three who had been domestic servants (Treasury Papers P.R.O. T. 1/632, 1513).

[9] A. M. Falconbridge, *Two Voyages to Sierra Leone 1791–93* (London, 1794), p. 57.

were usually transported to the West Indies or other settlements like Botany Bay. It may also well be that the Settlers themselves lured the women on board, and once on the ships, they decided to stay, for there is evidence that at least twelve of the women signed the Agreement to go to Sierra Leone.

Very little is known about the white men who went to Sierra Leone as colonists. Sharp mentions an agent-conductor, three surgeons, a chaplain, a land surveyor, a town-major and a gardener.[10]

A grant of land, twenty miles square i.e. 400 square miles, was obtained from King Tom, a neighbouring chief, for the use of the Settlers. The harbour was named St George's Bay, and the town, Granville Town, after Granville Sharp who had done so much for the Negroes. Sharp, however, in a letter to the inhabitants, dated 16 May 1788, addressed them as 'the worthy inhabitants of the province of Freedom, on the Mountains of Sierra Leone' – the earliest inspiration for the name Freetown.[11]

Unfortunately for the Settlers, there was not a sufficient time lapse between their arrival in May and the beginning of the rains in June for the erection of substantial dwelling houses. The result was that mortality in the first year was very high. In addition the settlement was depleted by emigration. Being pitched in an area where they were much sought after because of their western book learning, they were quick to take advantage of the situation and soon hired themselves out as clerks, etc., to the slave merchants in the adjacent regions.

When Sharp learnt of the reduction in the number of Settlers he became 'apprehensive that all the rest would be obliged to disperse in like manner, unless a speedy supply of live stock, with some recruits, could be immediately sent out'.[12] He decided to send this time chiefly white settlers, feeling that the Negroes from London had not shown the regularity or industry he had expected. In April 1788 Sharp chartered a vessel, the *Myro*, in which he shipped out provisions and thirty-nine passengers of whom the majority were white. Most of these newcomers defected to the slave merchants, presumably for higher wages. Otherwise the arrival of the vessel was a help to

[10] P. Hoare, *Memoirs of Granville Sharp* (London: Colburn, 1820), pp. 317 and 328.
[11] Ibid., p. 324.
[12] Ibid., p. 327, cf. Sharp's letter to the Settlers, 16 May 1788.

the straggling settlement. The Captain confirmed with King Naimbana the cession of land which had been made with King Tom in 1787.

In November 1789 the unprotected colony was attacked and burnt down by a neighbouring chief in retaliation for a similar injury inflicted on his town by the crew of an English ship-of-war. Having lost their homes and property, the colonists were dispersed throughout the country.

Thus ended the first attempt at founding a colony in Sierra Leone. On the whole, it was not a happy experience for the friends of the Negro in England. It seemed that the underlying philosophy of Granville Sharp and others was that once in Africa in their own soil, the Negroes would be capable of every advance which had been achieved by the England of their day. Thus, no attempt was made to strengthen the executive arm of government, and every colonist was given equal power in the administration of the territory. Indeed, this lack of delegation of authority was in the end a disadvantage, for it was impossible to get co-operation from the inhabitants in the pursuit of any major task. They could not, for example, agree on a person to govern them, and made three appointments within one year.

It became clear to the group of philanthropists that two things above others were required if the settlement was to succeed; first, some legitimate commerce to take the place of the slave trade and, second, a better selection of colonists for the settlement.

In 1790 the St George's Bay Company was formed for the pursuit of an 'honourable trade with the coast of Africa'.[13] In 1791 the Company sent out as their agent Dr Falconbridge, with a commission to examine and report on the state of the colony and to afford a temporary relief to the Settlers until the grant of a charter would enable the Directors to take more effective and permanent measures for the prosperity of the settlement. Later that year, the Company was transformed into the financially much more powerful Sierra Leone Company and the trading interest was given pre-eminence. This is indicated by the leading rôle of the philanthropist, Granville Sharp, in the earlier Company compared to his correspondingly minor

[13] The Directors of the Company included Granville Sharp, William Wilberforce, the celebrated abolitionist, and Henry Thornton, the London Banker, cf. Wadstrom, vol. II, op. cit., pp. 224–5.

rôle in the Sierra Leone Company and the much more influential position of the banker Henry Thornton as Chairman of the latter Company.[14]

Falconbridge was able to bring together about sixty-four of the Settlers and they occupied a number of abandoned huts a few miles east of the original settlement, at the present Fourah Bay, which they renamed Granville Town. The Settlers, in the eyes of their benefactors, showed the same want of discipline and the same unco-operative spirit as had characterized the former settlement. Of them, Mrs Falconbridge wrote:

> I really think (we) have less to fear from them (the natives) than our own people, who are extremely turbulent, and so unruly at times, that 'tis with difficulty Falconbridge can assuage them, or preserve the least decorum.[15]

Because of past experience with Negroes from London, the Company continued to refuse them passage. The Company sent instead Europeans both as colonists and for the administration of the colony. The Report of the Sierra Leone Company for the year 1791 states that 'in all there went out in that year 119 white persons. . . .'[16]

No preferential treatment was given to the whites. The Officers of the Company were particularly instructed to secure

[14] Cf. 1st Report of the Sierra Leone Company. 'The directors are endeavouring, in the outset, rather to lay the foundation of the happiness of Africa, and of future prosperity to the company, than to grasp at any premature advantages. But they trust that they are not too sanguine in looking forward to considerable and growing profits, resulting from, and connected with, the increasing prosperity of the country under their jurisdiction.' Wadstrom, vol. II, op. cit., p. 23.

In trying to sell shares in the Company, Clarkson wrote: 'I should not permit anyone to become a purchaser, who would not be better pleased with the good resulting to Africa than from great commercial profits to himself; not that the latter may not be expected; but in case of a disappointment, I should wish his mind to be made easy by the assurance that he has been instrumental in introducing light and happiness into a country where the mind was kept in darkness and the body nourished only for European chains.'

'In the election of Company's officers,' wrote Hoare, 'the compliment, often paid to Mr Sharp on other occasions, of placing him in the chair, was here omitted, as the philanthropic object of the settlement had by many been deemed so highly visionary, that it was judged advisable to elect a chairman, whose ordinary connections with concerns of more acknowledged substantial foundation might seem to authorize the expectation of success. The person chosen was the late Henry Thornton, Esq. afterwards Governor of the Bank.' Hoare, op. cit., p. 364.

'Roughly the balance seems to have been preserved between profit seeking and philanthropy.' E. C. Martin, *The British West African Settlements 1750–1821* (London: Oxford University Press, 1927), p. 113.

[15] Falconbridge, op. cit., p. 60.

[16] *Report of the Sierra Leone Company, 1794*, pp. 7 and 37.

to all blacks and people of colour at Sierra Leone, equal rights and equal treatment in all respects, with the whites. They were to be tried by jury and the Council were instructed to allot to the Negroes employments suited to their present abilities and to afford them every opportunity of cultivating their talent.

The Directors had contemplated sending further shiploads of white colonists, but the high mortality among the earlier colonists and the prospects of recruiting free Negroes altered their decision. The possibility of the additional resource of new colonists was connected with the arrival in London from Nova Scotia of a Negro, Thomas Peters, to plead the cause of those Negroes who had been transplanted to Nova Scotia. In London he came in contact with the promoters of the Sierra Leone venture, who, no doubt, told him of their settlement. The possibility of strengthening the colony with new recruits was most welcome to the Directors, and with their help, Peters was able to present a Memorial to the then Secretary of State, the Hon. Mr Grenville, in which he stated the grievances of his people in Canada and asked for some redress.[17]

The Negroes, known generically as Loyalist Negroes, who came into the province of Nova Scotia after the American War of Independence, consisted of freedmen as well as slaves. Some had entered as the slaves of their loyalist masters, though they were classified as 'servants'. Others had fought as soldiers in the Black Pioneer Corps or as buglers and musicians in nearly every loyalist corps. These were settled as disbanded soldiers in Halifax and other parts of the province.

Peter's Memorial was quickly considered by the Secretary of State and in his letter of 6 August 1791 to Governor Parr of Nova Scotia, he requested the latter to investigate the charges complained of by Peters and to make an offer to transport to Sierra Leone at Government's expense those of the Negroes who wished to depart. In his reply of 27 September, the Governor informed Mr Secretary of State that he had 'already appointed persons fitting the purpose, with proper instructions to inform the Black people of the intended settlement at Sierra Leone'.[18]

[17] A. Archibald, 'Story of Deportation of Negroes from Nova Scotia to Sierra Leone', *Coll. of the Nova Scotian Historical Society, Halifax*, vol. VII (1889–91), p. 135.

[18] *Canada, Public Archives of Nova Scotia*, vol. XLVIII (Letters to Secretary of State, 1789–94).

It was necessary to send some understanding person, preferably an Englishman, to Nova Scotia to inquire into the situation of the Negroes, and to ease things, and if necessary to supervise the arrangements for their removal since the Nova Scotian Government was sensitive about criticisms of its policies towards the Negroes. For this work, Mr John Clarkson, a lieutenant in His Majesty's Royal Navy and brother of the abolitionist Thomas Clarkson, volunteered his services which were accepted by the Company. He was armed with instructions on how to proceed and the terms on which persons will be accepted in the new colony. Each person having a certificate signed by Mr Clarkson or his assistant, Mr Hartshorne, testifying to the honesty, sobriety and industry of the bearer was to receive a grant of land at Sierra Leone, subject only to such conditions as shall be imposed on all Settlers, black as well as white. The Directors were particular in making explicit that the Colony would be free from all forms of racial discrimination.[19]

About the people who volunteered for Sierra Leone, Clarkson wrote:

I have every reason to believe that the majority are men of good moral characters. I remarked how fearful the whole were of getting into debt and that they questioned me closely relative to the assistance to be given them to support their families at Sierra Leone without borrowing money.[20]

In a letter to Henry Thornton, Clarkson referred to the inhabitants of Preston, one of the Negro townships in Nova Scotia, in the following manner:

I can assure you that the majority of the men are better than any people in the labouring line of life in England. I would match them for strong sense, quick apprehension, clear reasoning, gratitude, affection for their wives and children, and friendship and goodwill towards their neighbours. If I speak more favourably of these men than the rest, it may be because I have seen more of them, as they live in this neighbourhood, but I have good grounds for having formed a favourable opinion of the whole.[21]

[19] The terms stipulated that 'every free black . . . shall have a grant of not less than twenty acres of land for himself, ten for his wife, and five for every child'. It is significant that the 'Terms of the Sierra Leone Company, to all such Settlers as shall sail from England, in order to go to Sierra Leone' provided the same grant for the white Settlers, cf. Wadstrom, op. cit., vol. II, p. 228.

[20] J. Clarkson, 'Mission to America', *Public Archives of Nova Scotia*, MSS., p. 51.

[21] Ibid., p. 176.

Throwing more light on his own attitude and his instructions to the coloured population, Clarkson wrote in another letter to Thornton dated 1 December 1791:

> I have told the men that I shall form a very unfavourable opinion of those who may show an inclination to be servants to any gentlemen, when they have an opportunity of becoming their own masters, and valuable members of society if they please, and that in short, the character of the black people for ever after will depend on the manner they conduct themselves, and that the fate of millions of their complexion will partly be affected by it.[22]

It is tempting to conjecture how much they were flattered and impressed by this piece of advice. This may have contributed to the aversion they subsequently developed towards manual work, and their own faith in their intrinsic worth and superiority.

Clarkson also gave some very pointed advice on the way in which the settlement was to be ordered, which, in the light of subsequent events, is of significance:

> The people are taught to believe from me that they are to become Men, and that no distinction is to be made between them and the whites . . . if that should take place without an immediate check, they will be disgusted and begin to doubt the sincerity of the Company's intention; but the worst of all would be setting a bad example. Begin well at first, and there is a chance of continuing; but if a bad example is set in the infancy of the Colony, I know not what may be the consequence.[23]

At last Clarkson's mission to this part of America was accomplished, and on the 15 January 1792 his fleet of fifteen vessels containing 1190 Negroes set sail for Sierra Leone. Sixty-five died on the passage and the remainder arrived at intervals from 28 February to 9 March 1792.

Clarkson records that two days before their arrival in Sierra Leone they passed another ship, the *Mary of Bristol*, bound for Anamabo for slaves. This simple reference underlines the peril of those days and the courage and faith of those who had dared to take others to the shores of Africa on a promise of freedom and racial equality.

[22] Ibid., p. 211. [23] Ibid., p. 213.

Clarkson soon learnt that the Directors of the Company had decided to establish a government by a council of eight men, of whom Clarkson was to be the Superintendent with no extra powers except a casting vote in the deliberation of the Council. This was a great disappointment to Clarkson, but as he records in his journal:

> Knowing that there could not be any people in existence, in every point of view, better calculated for forming a new settlement, than those I brought with me from America, if properly managed, and being convinced from what little I have already seen of the natives of Sierra Leone, that an honest, open, conciliatory, yet firm conduct towards them would in time encourage them to place a confidence in the purity of our intentions etc. Feeling additionally impressed with the conviction that if I left the Colony inevitable ruin must be the consequence, I was compelled to sink all private considerations, and agree to remaining here; and though I may be disgraced by blending my services with those of others, over whom I have no proper control, I have made up my mind to take the consequences, and accept the Government under its present objectionable form, and to remain with the poor Nova Scotians till the Colony is established or lost.[24]

Clarkson gives a list of the names of Negro families that embarked for Sierra Leone from Nova Scotia. It includes names like Samuel Wright, George Carrol, Jeremiah Davies, Pompey Campbell, Thomas Jones–surnames which became of common use in Freetown.[25]

After a delay of about a fortnight arising from a lengthy discussion with the indigenous Africans, the spot where the 'Black Poor' had settled was thought best for the intended colony. In a few more weeks, the site of the town was cleared and building began. In accordance with instructions, the town was named Free Town.

On 2 August, Clarkson sent the following message to the 'Freeholders of Granville Town':

> As we are now ready to lay out the lots of land for the different people of Free Town, I cannot suffer them to draw their lots without giving you an opportunity of partaking of the same chance. I am ready to receive you under our protection, provided you agree to

[24] J. Clarkson, op. cit., pp. 438–9. [25] Ibid., p. 237.

our law, and to consider you with the same tenderness as those I brought with me from America. I am determined to forget everything that has passed, and consider you and our people as one. If you will behave well, I will do my utmost to promote your happiness, and therefore, I hope we shall live in perfect harmony together.

Having obtained a satisfactory reply he wrote on 4 August:

I have just received your letter, and am happy to find such a likelihood of unanimity and harmony between the Freeholders of Granville and Free Town. It gives me heartfelt satisfaction to find that we are likely to get into some kind of order, and hope we may begin under the blessing of God to date our happiness with that of your posterity from this hour. I shall from this day consider the inhabitants of Granville and Free Town as brethren . . .[26]

Thus the remnant of the first Settlers became merged in the much larger body of Negroes who had been transferred from Nova Scotia, and the subsequent records seldom make a clear or consistent distinction between the two groups after this date.

One of the priority tasks of the Freetown government at this stage was the distribution of land, which they found more difficult than was originally expected. They could not give each man the twenty acres promised, and each had to accept four acre lots instead. This was naturally disappointing to the Nova Scotians who had left Canada primarily because of a failure of fulfilment of earlier promises by the British. Further, the Nova Scotians regarded the annual quit rent which the Company requested them to pay as an added breach 'of that assurance upon the faith of which they had been induced to emigrate', for Clarkson had promised them before they left Canada that they would not need to pay any rents in Sierra Leone.[27] These early obstacles over land no doubt contributed to the marked preference of the Settlers for occupations other than husbandry for their sons. Indeed similar reasons were adduced before the Committee of Inquiry into the State of the Colony in 1827 to explain and justify the state of neglect in which their lots of land were allowed to remain.[28]

[26] Ingham, *Sierra Leone after a Hundred Years*, pp. 102–3.

[27] *Great Britain, Parliamentary Papers*, vol. VII, cf. (Report of the Commissioner of Inquiry into the State of the Colony of Sierra Leone, 1827).

[28] Ibid.

Wadstrom gives a description of Freetown as it was about this time, i.e. 1793. He wrote:

> Much of the industry of the colonists has been applied to the building of the town. It is situated on a dry and rather elevated spot, on the south side of the river, and occupies between 70 and 80 acres, its length being about one third of a mile, and its breadth nearly the same. It contains near 400 houses, each having one twelfth of an acre annexed, on which a few vegetables are raised. There are nine streets, running from N.W. to S.E. and three cross streets, and they are 80 feet wide, except one, which runs within 50 feet of the river, and which is 160 feet wide. In the broad street area, are almost all the public buildings, consisting of a church, near the middle, capable of containing 800 people; a Governor's house and offices; a large store-house, under which, and the governor's house, there are brick store-cellars; a large hospital, and 6 or 8 other wooden houses, offices and shops, occupied by the Company's servants. The frames of all these buildings went from England. . . . The houses of the colonists were at first inferior, but are now far superior to those of the natives. A few have been repaired and enlarged; but most of them have been rebuilt, the general site having been changed by the government. The lots given to the Nova Scotians lie on the S.E. of Freetown, all the western district being possessed by the natives, and the southern being thought too mountainous for present cultivation. . . .[29]

The streets were given characteristically English names by Governor Thompson which they still retain, like Wilberforce, George, Charlotte and Gloucester. The plan on page 32 shows Freetown as it was in 1815 with the names of the principal streets and the allotments of the Settlers. In the legislative sphere, an old Anglo-Saxon system of local government of 'frank-pledge' was introduced. Every ten families were grouped into a tithing over which there was a tithing-man, and every ten tithings formed a hundred over which there was a hundredor. At this time there were three hundredors who were consulted by the government in cases which concerned the interests of the Nova Scotians.[30]

Certain references in the reports of the Directors give some indication of the position and imagery of the Nova Scotians. The following incident illustrates the incipient image the Nova

[29] Wadstrom, op. cit., vol. II, pp. 60–2.

[30] Great Britain, Public Record Office, Colonial Office, *Dispatches and Reports*, Series No. C.O. 270/2 (hereinafter cited as C.O. with the appropriate number).

Scotians were entertaining of themselves. Wadstrom reports that:

When the governor and council dismissed one of them for disrespect to his superiors, a number of them formally applied to have a law established, that no Nova Scotian working for the Company should in future be turned off, unless after a verdict by a jury of his peers. Allowing at last, that a part of the Company's own land near the shore, should be reserved for public uses, some of them conceded the point, by saying, that they would *oblige* the Company with the piece of land. . . . It is worthy of remark that they usually prefer [sic] these and all their other claims, though matters of contract between the two parties, emphatically as freemen.[31]

The Directors were able to excuse this kind of behaviour. They reported in partial extenuation:

In estimating the whole character of the Nova Scotians, their past condition ought not to be over-looked. It should be remembered that all of them were once slaves; that, like others in the same state, they were probably little restrained in many branches of morals. Their faculties were then degraded, their opportunities of knowledge small, and they had little inducement to cultivate their intellects. Doubtless they strongly felt their hardships; but they probably know little of the true nature of civil rights; and, we may suppose, often confounded the unavoidable evils of life, and the punishments needful in society, with the ills imposed by arbitrary power; for accurate discrimination can signify little to men involved in hopeless captivity. To the want of such discrimination, and not to any moral or intellectual defect, much of their unreasonableness, and some of the absurdest of their claims, are obviously traced.[32]

The Directors concluded:

Let it therefore, be carefully remembered, that everything said against the character of the N. Scotians, must be understood with various exceptions and limitations; and that, the turbulence of some, and the unreasonableness and jealousy of many of them, are more or less to be looked for, in any body of men, who have been so unfavourably circumstanced. Their faults are not incident to them as blacks, but as men. And who will say, that, if he had struggled through a like succession of vexations, hardships and disappointments, his character would not have been marked by the same prejudices and untoward dispositions, which belong to some of the present colonists of Sierra Leone?

[31] Wadstrom, op. cit., vol. II, p. 68.

[32] Ibid., p. 70.

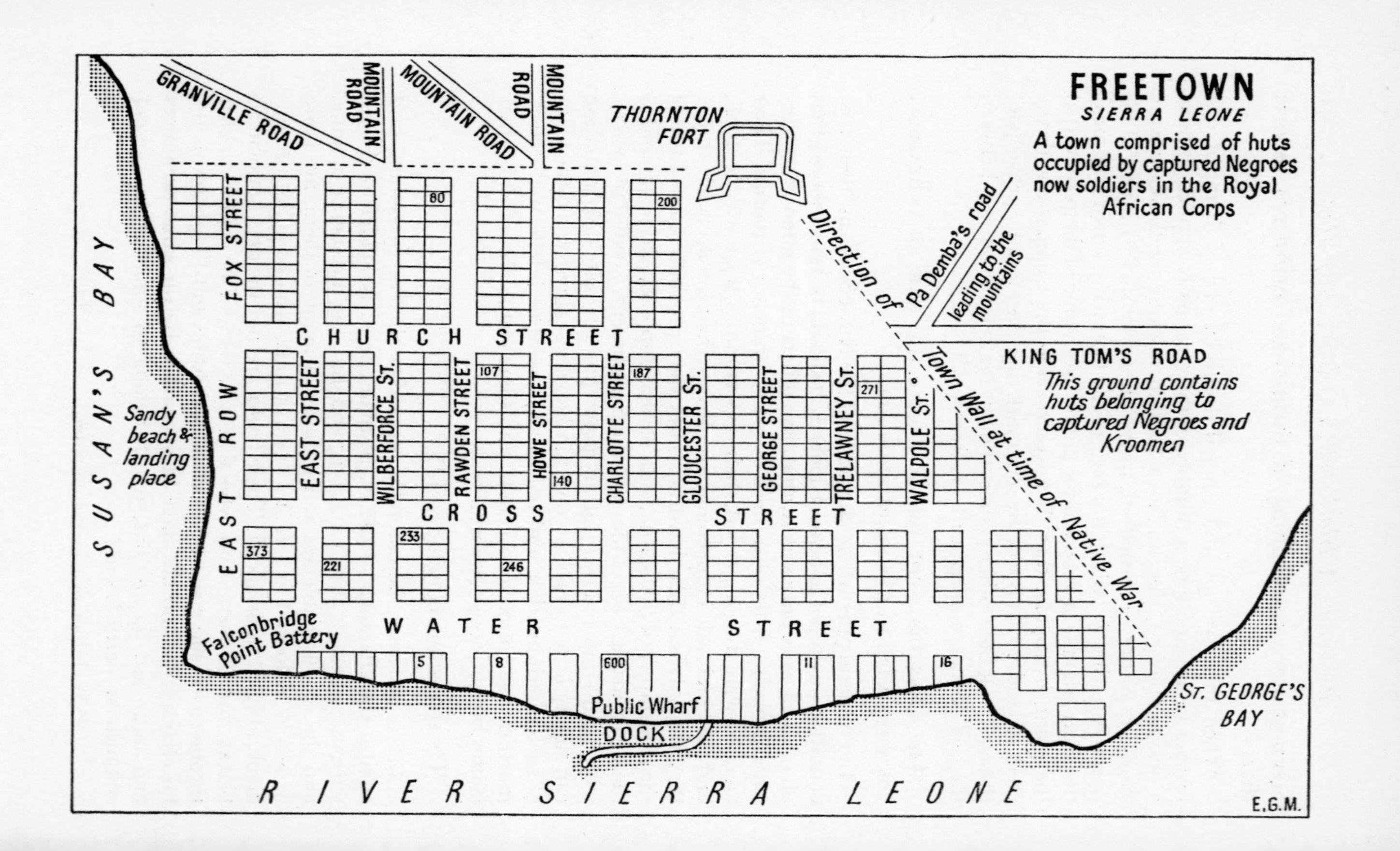

FREETOWN
SIERRA LEONE
A town comprised of huts occupied by captured Negroes now soldiers in the Royal African Corps
GRANVILLE ROAD
MOUNTAIN ROAD
MOUNTAIN ROAD
MOUNTAIN ROAD
THORNTON FORT
Direction of Town Wall at time of Native War
Pa Demba's road leading to the mountains
KING TOM'S ROAD
This ground contains huts belonging to captured Negroes and Kroomen
FOX STREET
CHURCH STREET
EAST ROW
EAST STREET
WILBERFORCE ST.
RAWDEN STREET
HOWE STREET
CHARLOTTE STREET
GLOUCESTER ST.
GEORGE STREET
TRELAWNEY ST.
WALPOLE ST.
CROSS STREET
WATER STREET
80
200
107
140
187
271
373
221
233
246
5
8
600
11
16
SUSAN'S BAY
Sandy beach & landing place
Falconbridge Point Battery
Public Wharf
DOCK
RIVER SIERRA LEONE
ST. GEORGE'S BAY
E.G.M.

The Directors propose to spare no pains nor expense to maintain this important part of their establishment on the best footing and to this object, they will direct the peculiar attention of the government. For to this rising generation of well educated blacks, they chiefly look for the gradual improvement of the colony. To them also, it seems not presumptious to hope, that the more distant and even interior parts of Africa, may one day own Christianity, knowledge and civilisation.[33]

Thus we find the policy of the Company already set to use this group of people as the germinal seed for future developments in Africa. They were provided with schools, medical facilities and all other means that would help them to qualify for the opportunities that were ahead. The Nova Scotians in turn made use of these facilities and with time developed an image of themselves in which they regarded these facilities not as a privilege but as a duty owed them as of right. Moreover, their preferential treatment made them feel socially superior to the native Africans around them. Thus at this very early stage the society was already structured into two main classes of 'Settlers' and 'Natives' depending on ascriptive criteria.

The fourth sizeable group of colonists to arrive from the western world were the Maroons in 1800. These were former slaves in the West Indian island of Jamaica, who had wrested freedom for themselves and who in the subsequent skirmishes with the British forces, were lured into laying down their arms, and, instead of the amnesty they had hoped, were shipped to Nova Scotia.[34]

Apart from these groups of settlers, a number of native immigrants had trickled into the Colony during this early period. Some had come as labourers; others for the purposes of trade.[35] Others had stayed on their farms and villages, as the authorities were unable to allocate or bring under use all the lands ceded.

Thus there were at this time in the colony (excluding the officers of the Sierra Leone Company), a few white colonists, the Nova Scotians, the Maroons and the indigenous tribal groups residing in the small hamlets dispersed throughout the settlement. With social differences also went geographical and

[33] Wadstrom, op. cit., p. 74.

[34] C. Dallas, *The History of the Maroons* (London: Longman and Rees, 1803).

[35] *Minutes of Evidence before a Committee of the House of Commons respecting African Slave Trade 1790*, pp. 167–8.

spatial distinctions, for the two main groups, the Nova Scotians and the Maroons, were each quartered in different parts of the town.

For many years the colonists were maintained in addition to the local foodstuffs by a supply of provisions and stores from England. Provisions included beef and pork, biscuits and cheese, flour, oatmeal, barley and butter. In religion the Settlers were predominantly Wesleyans, Baptists or members of Countess of Huntingdon's Connexion. Their church organizations were not simply religious institutions. They were also centres of the social life of the community: they provided a field of activities in which the free Negro could acquire status and exercise leadership.

The picture, then, in 1807, was that of a small community, coloured in complexion, living a life as near as possible to what their benefactors expected of them. The standards they set themselves in dress, in food habits, in speech, were western standards. They did not mingle socially with the indigenous Africans around them with whom they felt they had nothing in common. In fact, they were not encouraged to mix. They prided themselves on their knowledge of the English language, and this language dissimilarity from the rest of the population was a further factor in keeping the groups apart.

This consciousness of themselves as alien to all around them and the corresponding assumption that their way of life was the best and the standard to be copied, was enhanced by the fact that they had the full backing of the English administration and British prestige. The Settlers were looked upon, not as subjects to be colonized, but as active and equal partners in the business of British colonization. Their benefactors had laid upon this band of men 'the honourable office of introducing to a vast country long detained in barbarism, the blessings of Industry and Civilization . . . and of imparting . . . the light of Religious Truth and the security of the comforts of Civilized Society'.

Thus the first stage in the evolution of social stratification in Freetown was characterized by a class structure in which ascriptive distinctions rather than achievements, like occupation and income, played the decisive rôle in status ranking. In this first stage Settler descent–an ascriptive criterion–was the fundamental factor that opened the opportunities for achievement in all other spheres.

Chapter 4

ARRIVAL OF LIBERATED AFRICANS 1807–1850

THE abolition of slavery gave the philanthropists and liberals another reason for supporting the Sierra Leone venture. Freetown was now to be the home for the many who would be manumitted before they completed the old 'middle passage' journey. During over half a century, over 40,000 Negroes were thus freed and settled in Freetown. Both the Christian agents and the Government regarded it as their duty to bring the benefits of western civilization to these new immigrants. Their efforts did not go unrewarded. The Liberated Africans, as these recaptives were called, responded with vigour, and, within a generation, a number of them had progressed, first economically, and then socially, to win for themselves a place in the Settler hierarchy. In this chapter we shall trace the development of the society from the arrival of the first Liberated Africans to the position it had reached in about 1850 when the neat position of status ranking no longer held true because of this successful challenge by the Liberated Africans of the ascriptive basis on which the discrete social classes had been structured.

Four events occurred at the beginning of this period which were of tremendous consequence for the future of the young settlement. In 1807 the British Parliament passed into law a bill making the slave trade illegal within the British Empire. And, in April of that year, a philanthropic society, The African Institution, was formed, having for its object the moral and physical regeneration of Africa. It was composed mainly of the members of the Sierra Leone Company who were about to hand over the affairs of the Colony to the British Crown. Through the new society, they attempted to continue to exercise interest and influence in the colony. Thirdly, on 1 January 1808 Sierra Leone passed from the jurisdiction of the Sierra Leone Company to that of the Crown and became a Crown Colony.

The fourth event was the Order in Council of 16 March which established a Vice-Admiralty Court in the Colony for the trial and adjudication of all captured slaves brought in as prizes. Sierra Leone thus became the depository of Africans from all parts of the West Coast and beyond. The population of the settlement, which in 1807 was about 2,000, rose to about 45,000 by 1850, due in a large measure to this importation.

The term, Liberated African, is used here and in the literature, to refer to these Africans who were brought to Freetown while on their way to slavery in the New World, and released by decision of the Court of Vice-Admiralty or the later Court of Mixed Commission, which was established to try captured suspect slave ships and to release their human cargo if the slavers were found guilty of illicit slave trading.

Most of the Negroes were taken off slavers operating in the Nigerian creeks, but, as has been observed, the Negroes themselves came from as far north as Senegal and as far south as Angola, though the majority were from Yoruba and Ibo land in Nigeria.

The policy of the Government towards the new arrivals varied with each successive Governor. Mr Kenneth Macaulay, a European trader in the colony and a cousin of Zachary Macaulay, summarized the position in the two decades before 1827 in his pamphlet, *Sierra Leone Vindicated*, as follows:

The Colony has been grievously injured by the want of a systematic plan or rule for its government. Every Governor has been left to follow his own plans, however crude and undigested; and no two Governors have ever pursued the same course. This remark applies more particularly to the management of the Liberated African. Mr Ludlam pursued the system of apprenticing them; Mr Thompson set that aside, and turned them loose in the Colony, without any general superintendence other than its general policy. Captain Columbine employed them on the public works or apprenticed them. Colonel Maxwell, after delivering over to the persons appointed to receive them, all the men fit for His Majesty's Service, apprenticed a part of the remainder and then commenced forming villages with those who could not be disposed of. Sir Charles MacCarthy gave up apprenticing, except in particular cases, and adopted the plan of forming them into villages under such civil superintendence and religious instruction as he could command, keeping the youths and children in schools, or making mechanics of them; neglecting perhaps too much, in his successful attempt to make them orderly and quiet citizens, the equally desirable object of making them industrious agriculturists and growers of exportable produce.[1]

Three of these policies, viz. apprenticing individuals, enlistment in the army, formation of villages, played a significant part both in the process of adjustment of the Liberated Africans to the Freetown situation and as agencies in the socialization of the newcomers to the dominant culture status of the Settlers.[2]

The apprenticeship system set the stage for the later fosterage or adoption of children which formed a central feature of Freetown society from its earliest days. Those who were apprenticed in the homes of Settlers were able to learn how to behave in the ways of the favoured group. Service in a higher class home has always had socializing functions and provided opportunities for getting ahead. The Bible gives the story of Joseph, who rose from the position of servant of Potiphar to become ruler of all Egypt, second only to Pharaoh himself. Hecht, in his *Domestic Servant Class in Eighteenth Century England*, has shown how English servants were able to rise in the social scale by taking advantage of what they could learn of 'better' behaviour in their master's homes. Some of the Liberated African children passed from apprenticeship to adoption and were given the family name of the respective Settler family. Others took the family names of their masters, though they were never adopted, and remained domestics in the respective households.

Enlistment in the army also contributed to the socialization process. According to an Order in Council of 16 March 1808, the Collector of Customs had to surrender to the military and naval authorities all captured slaves whom he considered fit for service as soldiers, seamen and marines. But the policy could not be implemented as the military authorities were not prepared at that time to enrol Negroes. Approval, however, came in 1810, and in that year recruitment commenced.[3]

A form of conscription seems to have gone on until about the 1840s, though the records on this are at variance.

[1] K. Macaulay, *The Colony of Sierra Leone Vindicated From the Representations of Mr Macqueen of Glasgow* (London: Longman & Rees, 1827), p. 18.

[2] S.A. Walker, *The Church of England Mission in Sierra Leone* (London, 1843), p. xxx.

[3] J. J. Crooks, *Historical Records of the Royal African Corps* (Dublin: Simkin, 1902), p. 69.

K. Macaulay, op. cit., p. 12.

Colonel Denham, then Superintendent of the Liberated African Department, in his report of 14 May 1828 to the Under-secretary of State for the Colonies, R. W. May, noted that:

> With regard to the present practice of enlistment in the Royal African Corps, I have much satisfaction in being able to assure you, that it is much better conducted than you appear to imagine. The Africans are now fed for several days after landing, and comfortably clothed; and when they are a little reconciled to this new manner of treating them, soldiers or non-commissioned officers of their own country, are allowed to visit them for several days; and after the nature of the duties they will have to perform, as soldiers, have been perfectly explained to them, an officer attends, when, in my presence, those who have already mentioned to their countrymen their intention to enlist, turn out for the regiment.[4]

Here, as in the adoption situation, the Liberated Africans were faced with a way of life vastly at variance with their accustomed habits and dispositions to which they had to adjust.

The most deliberate socializing process, however, was carried on in the villages that were formed around the Settler settlement. By 1809 it was clear that more space would be required for the increasing number of Africans that were being brought to Freetown for adjudication and subsequent release. This periodic influx of recaptives to the Freetown community, where the Settlers had already set a standard based on western ideas of civilization, confronted the Government with a major social problem. Apart from colour identity, there was not much else that was common between the Settlers and the newcomers. The policy of apprenticeship was at this time under strong criticism on the grounds that those who were engaged in public works were treated as slaves and those who were adopted into Settler homes were being sold by their so-called guardians into slavery again. In August 1808 an Act was passed declaring the system of apprentices within the Colony to be illegal, null and void.[5] However, apprenticeship was to appear again as a means of disposing of the Liberated Africans.

In 1809 the first of the villages for Liberated Africans was formed in the mountain district of the Colony and was named

[4] Great Britain, *Parliamentary Papers*, vol. XXI (Papers relating to the Colony of Sierra Leone, 1830), p. 26.

[5] J. J. Crooks, *History of the Colony of Sierra Leone* (Dublin: Simkin, 1903), pp. 74–5.

Leicester. It was left to Governor Sir Charles MacCarthy (1814–24) to see clearly and logically the use to which the villages could be put and it was during his administration that the majority of them were formed. The decision as to the site for these villages was largely determined by the Government, but in some instances, as at Pa Sandi (later renamed Lumley) or at Congo Town, the Liberated Africans themselves were responsible for the choice. As Sibthorpe has written:

> These places were first founded by some of the Liberated Africans themselves, without direct orders from the Government; and generally, afterwards, the Government approved of their plans and enlarged the villages with greater numbers, at which time they were said to be properly founded; the suburbs of the capital insensibly arose in this way.[6]

MacCarthy concluded an arrangement with the Church Missionary Society by which that Society was responsible for the administration and cultural transformation of the Liberated Africans, the Government agreeing to subsidize their efforts. The position was in some ways comparable to the 'missi dominici' of the Carolingian era. In the eyes of the Carolingian kings, it will be recalled, to govern their subjects meant to imbue them with Christian morality. It was for this reason that they sought bishops as their counsellors and officials, and entrusted them with the function of 'missi'. The rôle of the missionary in the Liberated African villages was to make both citizens and Christians of the people. Baptism, wrote Governor MacCarthy, was 'an act of civilization'.[7] Western civilization and Christianity were, in the eyes of the administrators, complementary.

A Liberated African Department was established in Freetown to superintend and organize the disposition of the people as they arrived and to see to their welfare afterwards. Meticulous regulations were drawn up for their treatment. For example:

> They are to be maintained previous to location at the following rates–the healthy in the Queen's Yard, Freetown, at three half pence a day–the sick at Kissy Hospital, at two pence a day.
>
> But if their health and strength will permit, they are to be located

[6] A. B. C. Sibthorpe, *The History of Sierra Leone*, pp. 20 and 21.
[7] *Journal of W. A. B. Johnson*, p. 94.

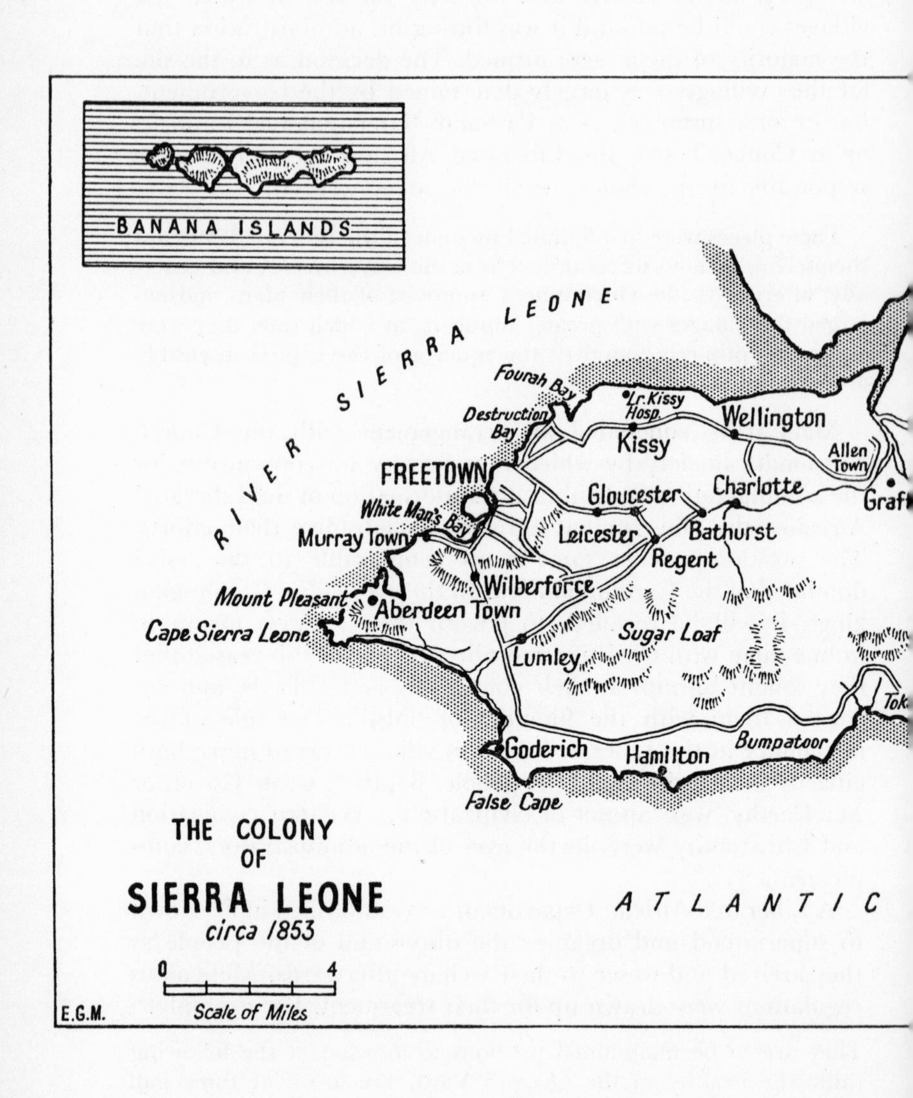
BANANA ISLANDS
RIVER SIERRA LEONE
Fourah Bay
Lr. Kissy Hosp.
Destruction Bay
Kissy
Wellington
Allen Town
FREETOWN
Gloucester
Charlotte
White Man's Bay
Leicester
Bathurst
Murray Town
Regent
Wilberforce
Mount Pleasant
Aberdeen Town
Cape Sierra Leone
Sugar Loaf
Lumley
Goderich
Hamilton
Bumpatoor
False Cape
ATLANTIC
THE COLONY OF SIERRA LEONE circa 1853
0
4
Scale of Miles
E.G.M.

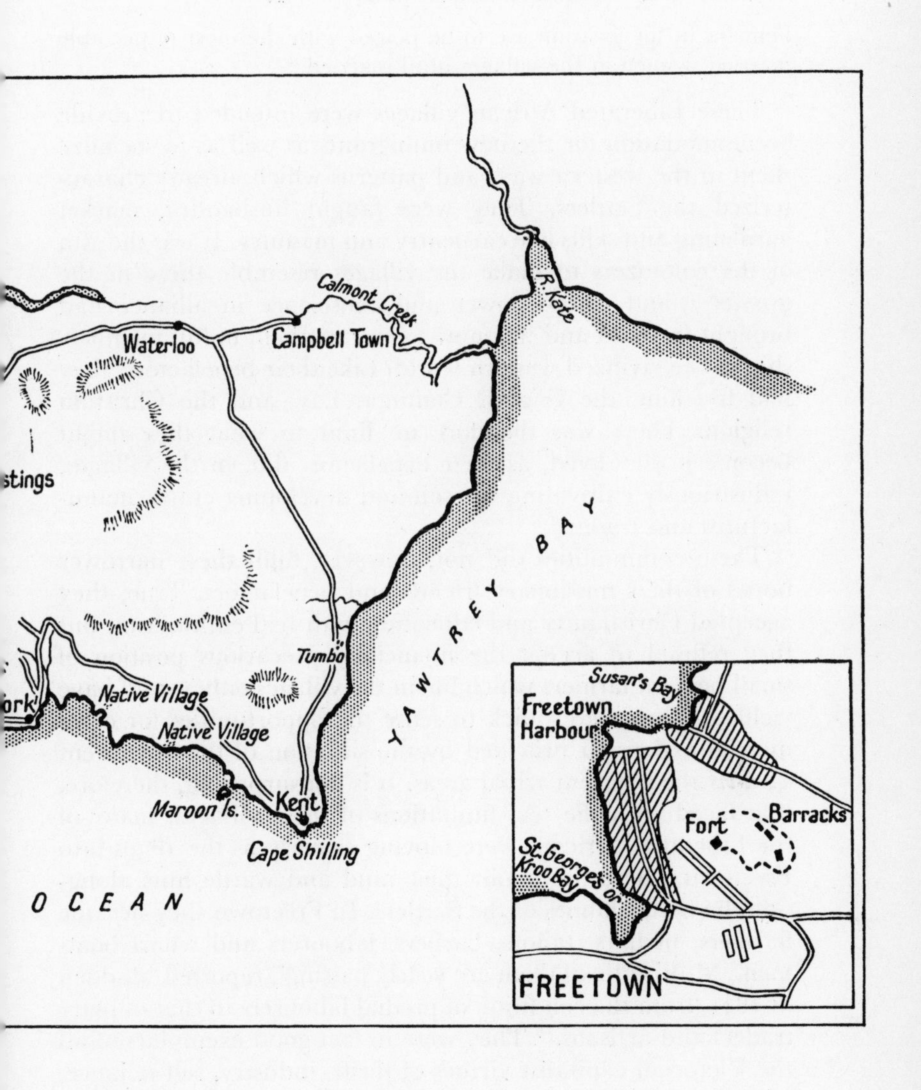
Calmont Creek
R. Kate
Waterloo
Campbell Town
stings
YAWTREY BAY
Tumbo
ork
Native Village
Native Village
Maroon Is.
Kent
Cape Shilling
OCEAN
Susan's Bay
Freetown
Harbour
Fort
Barracks
St. George's or
Kroo Bay
FREETOWN

without delay, unless, in the case of males, the labour of the strong should first be required for urgent public works.

Females fit for location are to be placed with the most respectable married women in the villages until married.[8]

These Liberated African villages were intended to provide accommodation for the new immigrants as well as to socialize them in the western ways and patterns which already characterized the Settlers. They were taught husbandry, market gardening and skills like carpentry and masonry. It was the aim of the colonizers to make the villages resemble those in the greater island whose power and conscience in alliance had brought freedom and was now to elevate them to full membership in the civilized western world. Like their benefactors, they had freedom, the English Common Law and the Christian religion. There was therefore no limit to what they might become if they lived, as their benefactors did, in the villages, industriously cultivating the soil and developing crafts, manufactures and trades.

These communities did not, however, fulfil these narrower hopes of their missionary friends and benefactors. True, they accepted Christianity and education with real enthusiasm, but they refused to accept the financially precarious position of small peasant farmers which life in the villages only would have yielded. They were quick to sense the opportunities for commercial expansion provided by the situation of the settlement *vis-à-vis* the adjacent tribal areas. It is not surprising, therefore, that faced with the real limitations of these villages, many of the Liberated Africans were moving as early as the 1830s into Freetown where they built their mud and wattle huts alongside the better homes of the Settlers. In Freetown they became hawkers, pedlars, tailors, barbers, labourers and wharf boatmen. 'Multitudes of them are yearly passing', reported Madden in 1841 'from the condition of predial labourers to that of petty traders and artisans.'[9] They were in fact good exemplars of all the Victorian capitalist virtues of thrift, industry, self-reliance, initiative and religious fervour. Had they remained in their villages as petty farmers as their critics wished they had done, they would never have proven their latent capacities and worth.

[8] C.O. 267/147, enclosures in Doherty 66, 24.9.1838.
[9] Cf. *Madden's Report 1841*. C.O. 267/172.

At first, i.e. until about the 1830s, there was not much contact between the Settlers and the groups of Liberated Africans in terms of social intimacy; there was a relationship of superordination and subordination which was encouraged by the Government and which was accepted on both sides. The Settler looked down upon the Liberated African as illiterate, heathenish and barbarous; the Liberated African, in turn, accepted as superior the culture of the Settlers and began to imitate those patterns of behaviour and attributes of the Settlers which connoted high status.

The social structure of Freetown at this time exhibited some features of a caste-like society. There was little association between members of the different groups, and the few relations permitted were severely limited and formally prescribed. Intermarriage between persons of the different strata was not approved and vertical social mobility was hardly possible.[10] Chief Justice Hogan, in a despatch to Earl Bathurst, dated 25 May 1816, noted:

> The pride and pretension of birth, and the vanity of fortuitous worldly distinctions nowhere produce more distant personal estrangement than the accidental differences which exist here create between the various descriptions of the same common stock of Africans, collected together for its own wise purpose through the inscrutable ways of Providence.[11]

From these and similar bits of evidence one can safely conclude that the gradations in Freetown society about the mid-century depended very largely on Settler descent and also on participation, and conformity to, western cultural patterns.[12]

Up to this time, the opportunities for social mobility had been limited to the Settlers. In the villages, the partnership between the Administration and the missionary society had provided just enough education to help the Liberated African adjust to the new way of life. But in Freetown, the spheres in which there could be equal participation or competition between Liberated Africans and Settlers were few.

[10] E. Melville, *A Residence in Sierra Leone*. Edited by Hon. Mrs Norton (London: John Murray, 1849), p. 21.

[11] Hogan to Bathurst, C.O. 267/43.

[12] Reference to the separateness of the two groups and the superior attitude of the Settlers towards the Liberated Africans abound in the literature. For additional sources, cf. M. Church, *Liberated Africans, In a Series of Letters from a Young Lady to her Sister in 1832–4* (London, 1835).

The most profitable avenue for advancement which lay open to the Liberated African in the Freetown environment was, therefore, trade. The openings with greater prestige, like government service and ownership of rent-yielding properties, were the monopoly of the Settlers. And so the Liberated Africans turned to commerce, first as petty traders and then as owners of capital. Gradually they were able, like the trading classes of England in the eighteenth and nineteenth centuries, to utilize the necessary tools for successful upward social mobility and to find acceptance in the small but exclusive group of Settlers either for themselves or for their children.

'Mary Church', in one of her letters written in the 1830s, records the case of Mrs Carew as a good example of Liberated African success. She wrote:

> She told me with very proper gratitude where it is due; that she always remembered from what she had risen; that she came here without a farthing, but that by God's blessing on her own industry, and the assistance of kind friends, that she had brought up a large family, and was at present 'very well in the world'; that her eldest daughter was going to be married, and that one of her sons was educating in London. She is a contractor for the soldiers rations, at least her name is always used.[13]

Sibthorpe underscored it more poignantly when he wrote about changes in the period around the 1840s as follows:

> The Nova Scotians saw with chagrin and envy themselves sinking into oblivion, and the 'captives', as they styled them, rising into influence and power. Instead of competition with those whom they deemed their inferiors, the Nova Scotians, with a few exceptions, withdrew from the field of industry in disgust, some transporting themselves back to America, some embarking in petty mercantile pursuits, where they were almost uniformly unfortunate through giving credit to the native beyond the jurisdiction of the Colony; these, without much thought of the future, living upon, the money acquired in their 'golden age', but none of them making any permanently strenuous effort to acquire more. Meanwhile, many of the emancipated blacks were rising by degrees to comparative eminence and wealth, partly by their own diligence and frugality, and partly through the favour shown them by the Colonial Government.[14]

[13] M. Church, op. cit., p. 39.
[14] A. B. C. Sibthorpe, *The History of Sierra Leone*, p. 134.

A number of these successful Liberated Africans decided to return to Nigeria from whence they came rather than remain in Freetown. In the Report on the *Blue Book* for 1841 it is recorded that:

Emigration to a certain extent (not transatlantic but from place to place along the shore) commenced in 1839 in the determination of a few Liberated Africans who had saved some money to purchase a vessel for the purpose of enabling them to revisit their own countries. . . . On the 1st April 1839, 67 persons embarked in the 'Queen Victoria' on the first exploratory voyage. The professed objects of this voyage were to determine how far a return to their own country would be compatible with those altered habits and desires which a lengthened observance of European customs and participation in British privileges had engendered and rendered familiar to them, and also to determine how far such return might be consistent with their expectations of a continuance of personal freedom.[15]

We read further that not only was the voyage a success, but that:

. . . two other vessels, the 'Wilberforce' and 'Free Grace', all owned by Liberated Africans have been purchased and are now engaged in the same sort of traffic. The gross number of persons who have emigrated in this manner is as near as can be ascertained about 500.[16]

While the missionaries viewed the emigration with approval and looked upon these people who had 'been habituated to the customs of civilized men and had participated in the privileges of the Christian Church' as the opening of a 'new, a welcome and unexpected avenue, for the extension of that cause' for which they, the missionaries, had devoted their lives, yet the effect of the emigration on the development of Sierra Leone as a whole was negative. The new bonds which were thus forged by the emigration to Nigeria meant that those who wished to adventure beyond the narrow confines of Freetown now had alternative and attractive contacts in Nigeria, and thus potential men for the interior were diverted to seek their fortunes along the coast. Later this coincided with Britain's expansionist plans, for when clerks, teachers and ministers were required for the new administrations in Nigeria, Gold Coast and elsewhere in

[15] C.O. 267/175, enclosed in Fergusson 12, 30.1.1842.
[16] Ibid.

the 1870s and after, the westernized Negroes in Freetown were on hand to fill the vacancies.

On 20 August 1853, an Act was passed in the British Parliament enacting that:

> All Liberated Africans domiciled or resident in the Colony of Sierra Leone or its Dependencies shall be deemed to be, and to have been for all purposes, as from the date of their being brought into, or their arrival in, the said Colony, natural-born subjects of Her Majesty, and to be, and to have been, capable of taking, holding, conveying, devising and transmitting any estate, real or personal, within the said Colony of Sierra Leone and its Dependencies.[17]

This removed all doubts about their rights to own land and property within the Colony or to be sued and tried in British Courts and eased the process of integration with the old Settler groups. Of course, the manifest intention behind the Act was not its integrative societal usefulness. Nevertheless this was one of its unintended and perhaps unanticipated consequences.

With the expansion in trade and the increasing participation of the Liberated Africans in the economic growth of the Colony, it was increasingly more difficult to maintain the old social distinctions based on status in the Weberian sense. Weber's thesis that 'every technological repercussion and economic transformation threatens stratification by status and pushes the class situation into the foreground' seems to be corroborated by the events in Freetown in the middle of the nineteenth century.

The people with wealth began to assume leadership in the various spheres of life and to validate their position by intermarrying with the old status groups and by displaying other forms of social success. Elements from the groups of Liberated Africans were pushing up the social ladder to form with the descendants of the Settlers the new upper class. As the opportunities were opened up to the Liberated Africans, as they became wealthy, western educated and Christian, the old distinctions began to be blurred, and by the 1870s were becoming almost obliterated.

Thus social stratification in Freetown had evolved through two stages. In this second stage, the structure was less crystal-

[17] 16 & 17 Vic., Cap. 16. Also J. J. Crooks, *History of the Colony of Sierra Leone*, op. cit., p. 189.

lized; we find the emergence of individuals with a fair amount of wealth but without the prestige or the education. We may illustrate this from the history of the Lewis family. In 1828 there was liberated in Freetown a cargo of captives from the Egba country of Nigeria. One of these Liberated Africans, a boy of about sixteen, was named William Lewis after the then Colonial Secretary, and sent to Murray Town, one of the Liberated African villages. For a time, Lewis was a fisherman after leaving the village school, but he left this occupation for the better opportunities in trade. He carried on trade with the interior, buying the foodstuffs which Freetown required and selling the European produce to the indigenous inhabitants in the interior of the country. In 1847 he was still described in an official document as a 'hawker', though he had prospered sufficiently to buy a store in Percival Street, Freetown, for £305. By 1859 he was living in the main thoroughfare of Oxford Street (Cross Street on map on page 32), the street where the best houses were situated, the heart of settler district. By 1870, Lewis was the owner of two small ships–the *Lewis* of forty-six tons and the *Mary* of twelve tons–which traded for produce. Of him, Hargreaves writes:

> Lewis now ranked among the principal merchants and public figures of the Liberated African community. He served in many offices and on committees, government and unofficial. In 1858 he was gazetted Lieutenant in the militia, and in 1862 he was Vice-President of the Mercantile Association to which both European and African merchants belonged. . . . He was a local preacher, a trustee of the new Wesley Chapel proposed in 1856, and a generous, if somewhat ostentatious contributor, to church funds.[18]

One of William Lewis' sons, Samuel, born 13 November 1843, was sent to Britain for his education and was called to the English Bar in 1871. He had a distinguished career in the legal and political fields in Sierra Leone, and was knighted by Queen Victoria of England on New Year's Day 1896, the first of his race to receive such honour. Of his marriage in 1874, his biographer, Hargreaves wrote:

> They were married in St George's Cathedral, probably because of the social esteem which the Established Church could command even

[18] J. D. Hargreaves, *A Life of Sir Samuel Lewis* (London: Oxford University Press, 1958), p. 5.

among its critics rather than from any attempt to find a middle way between the bride's Catholicism and the bridegroom's Methodism.[19]

This brief history illustrates the interaction of the different social factors which were influencing the process of social mobility in nineteenth-century Freetown. In a generation, the Lewis family had moved from the lower ranks of the class structure into the upper. They had moved by combining success, the accumulation of wealth, the acquisition of an honourable profession, a favourable marriage, and influential positions in Church and State. Once the opportunities were open to the Liberated Africans, Freetown could no longer remain a particularistic society where the privileges were only for the few of Settler descent.

The philanthropists had hoped that the new colony would not only permit the displaced persons of the Atlantic trade to evolve a society of their own, but that it would also prove an agency for the spiritual and social regeneration of the whole African world.[20] In this they were not ultimately to be disappointed. In a sense, of course, it could be said that Liberated Africans should have started with their own interior, which would have resolved their own position and contributed materially to the solution of one of the country's major social problems. Instead, they preferred to carry out the rôle of agency which the philanthropists envisaged, but they wanted to do it in their own way. Their kinship and sympathy for their brethren in Yoruba and Ibo land made them more conscious of the needs of that part of the continent, and Sierra Leone's loss became Nigeria's gain. Those who did not venture outwards preferred to merge with the old Settler groups into an exclusive oligarchical society.

During these mid-years of the nineteenth century, the ascriptive criteria decreased in importance as the opportunities for achievement were extended to the Liberated Africans. The first inroad was thus made on the caste-like structure of discrete status groupings which had characterized early Freetown.

[19] J. D. Hargreaves, op. cit., p. 20.

[20] For one statement of this standpoint, cf. the *Missionary Register*, August 1843, p. 356. 'We must not abandon, we must not neglect, this settlement of Sierra Leone. It is a great door, through which hereafter, the knowledge of the arts of social life will be communicated back, through the medium of the Negroes themselves, and disseminated over the shores of Africa, from whence they sprang.'

These developments were in fact a stage in the social evolution of the society from a structure made up of discrete status groupings to a continuum of economic and prestige classes. The latter position, in its purest form, was still to be attained, but in the middle years of the century, it was already possible for some individuals to improve their social class ranking through performance on achievement criteria.

Schematically the trend of the changes could be represented as follows:

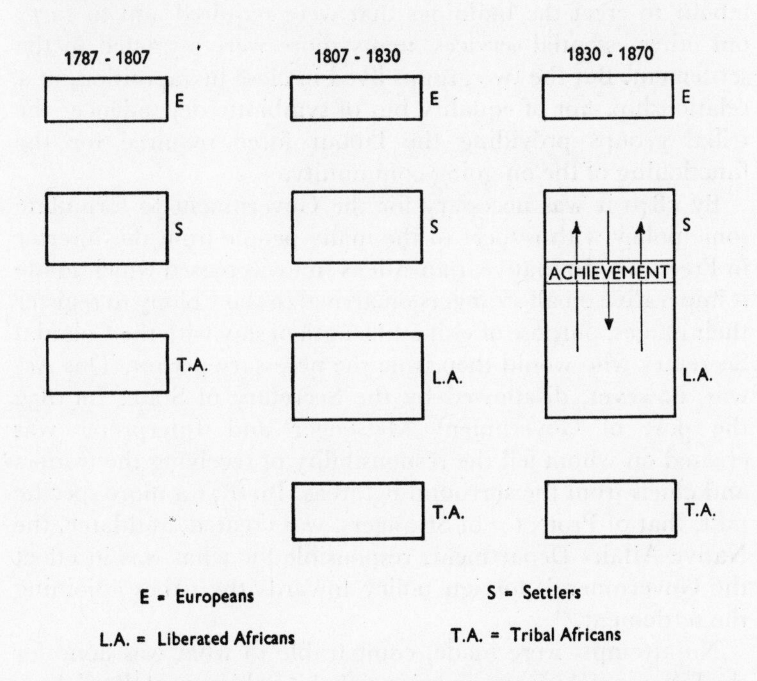

With the increase in the importance of achievement criteria as crucial determinants of social class position, the twin processes of upward and downward social mobility began to operate within two of the distinct groupings, i.e. the Settlers and the Liberated Africans. The Europeans continued to serve as a reference group for upwardly mobile individuals, but were in effect outside the status-power-reward system. The tribal individuals at least until the 1870s, were at the bottom of the scale, and could not participate effectively in the mobility process because they lacked the achievement criteria which could have rendered participation possible.

In actual fact, however, contact between tribal people and the Settlers had gone on from the very beginnings of the settlement. No attempt was made in those years to cultivate the whole of the ceded territory of twenty miles square, nor did the authorities insist on the evacuation of all indigenous inhabitants, though part was forcibly evacuated after the Temme attack on Freetown in 1789. Many remained, and with the demand for labour to erect the buildings that were required and to carry out other essential services, many more were attracted to the settlement. But the two groups lived in close juxtaposition, in a relationship, not of equality but of symbiotic dependence–the tribal groups providing the labour force required for the functioning of the on-going community.

By 1840 it was necessary for the Government to formulate some policy with respect to the many people from the interior in Freetown. In that year an Aliens Act was passed which made it imperative on all strangers on arrival in the Colony to register their names, purpose of visit and length of stay with the Colonial Secretary who would then issue the necessary permit. This Act was, however, disallowed by the Secretary of State. In 1852 the post of Government Messenger and Interpreter was created on whom fell the responsibility of receiving the traders and chiefs from the surrounding areas. In 1871 a more specific post, that of Protector of Strangers, was created, and later, the Native Affairs Department, responsible for what was in effect the Government's foreign policy towards the tribes adjoining the settlement.[21]

No attempts were made, comparable to what was done for the Liberated Africans, to bring tribal inhabitants of the Colony within the vortex of Settler society. Nothing was done to change the caste-like relationship between the tribal immigrants and the rest of the population.

[21] J. D. Hargreaves, 'The Evolution of the Native Affairs Department', *Sierra Leone Studies*, N.S., No. 3 (December 1954).

Chapter 5

PERIOD OF CREOLE ASCENDANCY 1850–1939

DURING this period the processes which we have noticed in Chapter 4 continued. The distinctions between Settler and Liberated African continued to disappear, and social position became structured increasingly on the basis of achieved criteria. By the 1920s, the polarities were no longer between Settler and Liberated African but between Creoles, as the descendants of both Settlers and Liberated Africans were called, and tribal Africans. Creole culture was given positive, while the tribal cultures were given negative, social value. The axis of subordination/superordination on which the society was built went unchallenged until the post-1920 period.

The term 'Creole' which refers primarily to the status grouping of Settlers and Liberated Africans and their descendants has had different meanings in different societies, and even its use in Freetown has undergone several changes. In the French West Indian Islands, for example, in the eighteenth century, the term referred to a person of French and Spanish descent born and reared in a colonial region as against the children who were sent to the metropolitan country for their education and training. In the United States, it has meant a white person descended from the French or Spanish settlers of Louisiana and the Gulf States, and preserving their characteristic speech and culture.[1] More generically, the term is used to refer to a person born of white and Negro parents.[2]

In the Freetown context the meaning of the term has varied. In the early period, it does not seem to have had a definite or consistent meaning. Mrs Melville, for example, used it to refer to Colony-born children of Liberated Africans.[3] Governor Macdonald applied it to 'mulatoes', presumably children of

[1] Cf. *Webster's New Collegiate Dictionary*.
[2] Cf. *Concise Oxford Dictionary*.
[3] Mrs Melville, op. cit., *passim*.

Settlers, and of Settlers and Europeans.[4] By the 1870s the term had come to mean Settlers, Liberated Africans and their descendants. The term was so used in the 1911 Census, and was so used to reconstruct the 1901 Census. By the 1930s the meaning of the term had expanded to refer to anyone sharing a number of western traits. As the Census Report for 1931 comments:

> There is a marked and growing tendency for the educated native to style himself 'Creole'. . . . A large number have been to Christian schools and, becoming Christians, adopt Christian names and lose identity with their tribes.[5]

In the past few years, however, this tendency has been on the decrease due in some measure to the growth of political and racial consciousness among the majority of the population.

It was left to the second generation children of Settlers and Liberated Africans to demonstrate the latent possibilities of the African and to redeem in some degree the wider hopes which the benefactors had placed in the original settlement at Sierra Leone.[6]

During this period, the Colony grew both numerically and spatially. It was in the 1870s a trader's city with a still expanding trade. In almost every walk of life there were trained or qualified Africans ready to exercise responsibility and make decisions. In 1872, Governor Pope Hennessey was able to recommend a transfer of more power to the Africans because he felt there were enough of them with the necessary qualifications to fill the posts in the Service. In his Despatch to the Earl of Kimberley, he wrote:

> Wherever it can possibly be done, I would strongly recommend dispensing with the service of Europeans on this coast. Fortunately this can be done, and to a greater extent than is generally imagined. It is no disparagement to the other members of the Legislative Council to mention the fact that the two ablest members of that body are both pure negroes. The best scholar on the coast–a man who knows Hebrew, Greek, Latin, French, German, Italian and Arabic and is well read in the literature of these languages–is Mr Blyden, a negro. The most intelligent clergy of the Church of England in the

[4] C.O. 267/221. [5] *Census Report 1931*, p. 46.
[6] Cf. Sierra Leone, *Annual Blue Book 1852*.

various settlements are the native pastors. Among the most trustworthy clerks in the public services are the native officials.[7]

The period 1870 to 1900 can indeed be called the apogee of Creole civilization and ascendancy. It was during this period that the Church Missionary Society's educational institution, Fourah Bay College, was affiliated to the University of Durham in England, and until the Second World War this was the only institution of higher education in West Africa where an individual could complete the requirements for a full university degree. The period also saw the reorganization of the municipality and the creation of a Mayoralty and Corporation analogous to the situation that had existed in the first period of crystallization when the Africans were responsible for a large part of the local government.

There was also during this period a vigorous and flourishing local press. Though official papers which printed both official documents and more general news had appeared as early as 1801, real newspapers did not emerge until the mid-century. In 1855 the first newspaper owned by a private individual, *The New Era*, was started by William Drape, a West Indian. By this time, many among the Freetown inhabitants had become thoroughly discontented with the constitution which gave the Governor and a small Council of his own choice the power of making laws, and *The New Era* voiced the grievances of this large section of the local population.[8] In 1862 a Mr Harleston of Nova Scotian descent put out *The Sierra Leone Weekly Times and West African Record* in which he attacked the Liberated Africans who were successfully undermining Settler exclusiveness. Thus while, by this time, the barriers between Settler and recaptive were already crumbling, there were those who were trying to stem the tide.

Fyfe, commenting on the press in the nineteenth century, writes:

The Newspapers of the 1850's and 1860's despite resounding names, were ill-written, carelessly produced, on poor paper with garbled, sometimes scarcely legible type. . . . The newspapers

[7] Pope Hennessey to Earl of Kimberley, 31 December 1872, *Colonial Possessions Reports 1873*, Part 11, 2nd Division, pp. 19–20.

[8] C. H. Fyfe, 'The Sierra Leone Press in the Nineteenth Century', *Sierra Leone Studies*, N.S., No. 8 (June 1957), pp. 226–36.

founded in the 1870's and 1880's set a higher standard. Rich Creoles like Sawyerr and Taylor could afford to buy better presses and paper; printers became more skilful. The contributors' style improved, reflecting the general increase of cultivation and fluency in a community where young men were no longer content to be shopkeepers like their fathers but were entering the learned profession.[9]

As was pointed out in the last chapter, the first involvement of the Liberated Africans in the Freetown society of the Settlers was in the economic order. Fyfe has shown in his article on 'The Life and Times of John Ezzidio' the astonishing development which was made by the descendants of the Liberated Africans during the period of Ezzidio's lifetime; indeed Ezzidio's history could be duplicated by that of many others in the Colony, as examples of the fullest realization of what became the Creole ideals and imagery of their rôle and destiny.[10]

Of him, Fyfe writes:

Remarkable as it is that a boy brought helpless, penniless, and friendless into a strange country should within a decade or so of landing be established in his own business, Ezzidio was only following very successfully the example many of his contemporaries were setting. Some started as servants or shopboys as he did. Others earned a little by fishing or cutting firewood. With their tiny capital they began trading in the streets, building up their pennies into pounds. . . . As there were no banks in the Colony, nor any industrial enterprise to invest in, small capitalists had to put their earnings into house property. They built houses, either to live in, and advertise their new splendour and credit, or to let. . . . Emmanuel Cline, for example, a recaptive from the Hausa country, spent over £600 buying good houses in Freetown between 1839 and 1845. . . . William Henry Pratt bought the lots on the north side of Oxford Street, between George and Trelawney Streets for £300, and built there a large house and shop . . . it was (and indeed still is) typical of Freetown, with its wealth so founded in house property, that

[9] C. H. Fyfe, 'The Sierra Leone Press in the Nineteenth Century', *Sierra Leone Studies*, N.S., No. 8 (June 1957), pp. 231 f.

[10] Cf. Ezzidio's testimony: 'John Ezzidio, General Merchant, 378 George Street, Freetown Sierra Leone.

I hereby certify that I am an African and have lived in the Colony for a period of 27 years, that I am engaged in business, importing into this place general merchandise amounting between three and four thousand pounds annually. That I carry on my own correspondence with brokers and merchants in England and that all my books and accounts are kept by native clerks who have been educated in the Missionary Schools, and whom after a little training I have found competent to keep my books . . .' C.O. 267/225. Enclosure in letter from Rev. H. Venn, 30.6.1851.

Sir Samuel Lewis

the rising class should quickly buy out the owners of the best houses.[11]

Another source of wealth was as contractors to the different Government departments. The newspaper *Artisan* for 8 August 1885 gives a list of successful business men who had started life as artisans.

The next stage was successful involvement and participation in the westernized status order of Freetown. This was made easier to accomplish when the Liberated Africans had come to accept the behaviour patterns and mores of the Settler society. Of Samuel Lewis, son of a recaptive and perhaps the most successful of his group, Hargreaves, his biographer, writes:

> Lewis's career provides an outstanding example of an African's successful response to the culture of western Europe, as received, for the most part, through the filter of colonial society. He entered into 'the blessings of Industry, and Civilization' in a way which might have satisfied the founding fathers of Sierra Leone. The really formative influences of his life had little to do with the cultures of tribal Africa, even as handed on through the Aku community of Freetown; though Lewis was known to express pride in his Yoruba ancestry, this was not a living force. His career was made among, and his character was moulded by, essentially 'Western' institutions – the English Bar, the Wesleyan Church, the business world of Freetown, the Legislative Council.[12]

The many mausoleums, sarcophagi, and vaults, the imported tombstones in the Freetown cemeteries, testify to the socio-economic position that had been attained by many families. A number of these memorials still stand to the many who helped to transform Freetown from its early humble beginnings in the late eighteenth and early nineteenth centuries to the thriving commercial centre and 'Athens of West Africa' it had become by the close of that same nineteenth century. These memorials serve as further evidence of the family ties that were being forged between the old aristocracy and the rising Liberated Africans.

Crystallization was reached when class and status were validated by political power. The political constitution which

[11] Fyfe, 'The Life and Times of John Ezzidio', *Sierra Leone Studies*, N.S., No. 4, pp. 214 f.

[12] J. D. Hargreaves, op. cit., p. 102.

was devised for the Colony in 1811 lasted with but minor changes throughout the period of territorial and numerical increase of the Colony. New territories were ceded or annexed, other parts of West Africa, like the settlements in the former Gold Coast, were for a time administered from Freetown; these changes, however, did not affect the political order. The Government continued to be in the hands of a Governor with the advice of a Council usually of seven members, all appointed by the Governor and almost all officials.

As the Colony expanded, many became discontented with the form of government in which they had no share. In 1850 the Rev. E. T. Poole, Colonial Chaplain, had published a book in which he protested against the Colony being ruled by a small secret council in which the people were not represented at all. In 1853 a Sierra Leone Committee of Correspondence was formed by Mr Lenaghan, a West Indian by birth practising law in the Colony, to press for 'the constitutional privilege of representation'.[13] In 1858 the Merchants' Association petitioned the Secretary of State for the Colonies to set up an elected House of Assembly in Sierra Leone.[14]

A political change was effected in 1863 when, under a new Charter, the old Council was divided into two – an Executive and a Legislative Council. The Executive Council was made up of officials while the Legislative Council was to include official, as well as unofficial, members. One of the two unofficial members was the successful businessman, John Ezzidio. His nomination was in effect the result of an election albeit on a most narrow franchise, by the Merchants' Association.[15]

Though the Colonial Office disapproved of this method of selection, succeeding Governors appointed Africans to serve as unofficial members after Ezzidio. In 1869 Governor Kennedy chose William Grant, another successful Freetown merchant. Although Grant was not elected by the community, he was

[13] C.O. 267/233, Kennedy Conf., 27 September 1853.

[14] C.O. 267/260, Hill 29, 17 February 1858.

[15] One unofficial member was Charles Heddle who had served in the old council from 1845. The Governor, Blackall, who had himself been a member of Parliament in England, was uncertain who to choose for the other, and decided it would be best to have him elected by the Mercantile Association. At the meeting held on 8 December 1863, there were present 14 Europeans, one Afro-West Indian, and 24 Africans. Two candidates, one European, John Levi, the other an African, John Ezzidio, were proposed. The voting was by secret ballot, and 23 votes were cast for Ezzidio and 13 for Levi.

regarded by the Governor as one who represented the people. In a despatch to the Governor, the Secretary of State for the Colonies wrote:

A Governor should choose not only those who are most likely to support Government, but those who will be taken to represent and will really inform you of the wishes of the intelligent portion of the community.[16]

After Grant, Henry Lumpkin and Syble Boyle were appointed; and in 1882, the most distinguished of them all, Sir Samuel Lewis, of whom we have written. (Cf. Chapters 4 and 11.)

In 1893 a comparable step to that in central government in 1863 was taken in local government when Freetown was created a municipality. In 1895 Sir Samuel Lewis was made its first elected Mayor.

From the 1840s onwards, a number of the descendants of both Settlers and Liberated Africans left Sierra Leone for other parts, particularly Nigeria and the former Gold Coast. Some went voluntarily to seek and make their fortune in foreign lands; others went as agents of Government, the Church, or the trading companies. 'They went', as Jones-Quartey puts it:

as accountants, clerks, teachers, ministers, and even top administrators without whom no modern processes or installations in those countries could have been worked.[17]

Of those that remained and their descendants who formed the resultant Creole community, Professor Macmillan wrote:

The Creoles, at any rate, like the better-class West Indians, are people with civilized standards. They are supported, moreover, in a feeling of superiority by the consciousness that, unlike the West Indians, they include no such traditionally dependent class as the great West Indian majority of plantation labourers–with the unfortunate consequence perhaps that they keep themselves aloof from the 'bush natives' who form a large and increasing part of the working population of Freetown.[18]

[16] C.O. 267/302, Draft Despatch answering Kennedy 233, 17.12.1869.
[17] K. A. B. Jones-Quartey, 'Sierra Leone's Role in the Development of Ghana 1820–1930', *Sierra Leone Studies*, N.S., No. 10 (June 1958), pp. 73ff.
[18] Meek, Macmillan and Hussey, op. cit.

Such was the standard which had been achieved by the Freetown of that day that thinkers like Edward Blyden could go so far as to regard Sierra Leone as the centre of the African race, the point from which western civilization and culture could spread and illuminate the surrounding areas.[19]

By the 1870s the process by which Settlers and Liberated Africans fused to form the new economic and prestige class of Creoles was well under way. Freetown once more displayed the concept of the well-knit community. Without using the language of the modern sociologist, Dr Blyden had concluded that in the last quarter of the nineteenth century, Freetown had again attained the quality of nationhood displayed during the régime of Governor MacCarthy, 1814–24.[20] Dr Blyden was thus calling attention to the second period of crystallization when status in Max Weber's sense was dominant. Or as Dr James Horton, another distinguished Sierra Leonean, wrote of his country in 1868:

> The inhabitants of the Colony have been gradually blending into one race, and a national spirit is being developed.[21]

It is not surprising that with material success and more stability came greater discussion of fundamental intellectual problems basic to Africa. For example, in 1868 Dr Horton had made a plea for the establishment of a university for West Africa. He wrote:

> Fourah Bay College should henceforth be made the University of Western Africa, and endowed by the Local Government, which should guarantee its privileges, and cherish the interests of literature and science in the Colony. A systematic course of instruction should be given to the students, and regius professors appointed.[22]

Rev. Henry Seddall, in his *Missionary History of Sierra Leone*, returned to this subject and added a new note. He wrote:

> That education has made wonderful progress in Sierra Leone no one can doubt who has read the newspapers there, the letters and

[19] E. W. Blyden, *West African University* (Freetown: Sawyerr, 1872), p. 14.
[20] W. W. Blyden, *Christianity, Islam and the Negro Race*, Second Edition (London, 1889), p. 235.
[21] J. A. B. Horton, *Western Africa–Vindication of the Negro Race* (London, 1868), p. 89.
[22] Cf. T. J. Thompson, *Jubilee and Centenary Volume of Fourah Bay College* (Freetown: Elsiemay, 1930), p. 51.

pamphlets of some of the leading native gentlemen of the Colony, and the sermons of some of the native pastors. Even the most cursory reader of these papers, pamphlets and sermons will perceive that there is springing up a most natural and very proper feeling of independence and nationality. Whilst acknowledging the immense debt of gratitude due to Europeans, educated Africans are beginning to long to slip away from their European leading strings, and they are proving themselves perfectly capable of discharging all their duties as citizens, and as Christians without foreign aid.[23]

Blyden and other notable contributors to the newspaper, *The Negro*, in the years 1872–4 were to argue that in future Africans should be educated by Africans and that the sentiments of Race and Nationality should be cherished and fostered.

The economic foundation of this society was based almost exclusively on trade. It is not surprising, therefore, that the intermittent depression of trade in the 1880s should have its repercussions on both the import and export trade of Freetown.[24] The merchants, in the circumstances, were not slow to look for the causes of their reverses in order to try and resolve their difficulties. Many attributed the adverse trade to the lack of control over the hinterland and the exposure of the settlement to the depredations of surrounding tribes. While wages fell, cost of living and immigration into the Colony from neighbouring tribal areas increased. There were many who were, therefore, ready to find a scapegoat and to regard the tribal people as the cause of their misfortune.

In a speech at a meeting of the Sierra Leone Association in 1886, A. J. Sawyerr was reported to have said:

There was a time in the annals of the settlement when a little Sierra Leonean might kick a Timeneh or Soosoo with impunity. Nowadays we hear of Timeneh 'strikes'. Significant phenomenon, gentlemen. We must not consider ourselves safe and secure because we have a regiment at the barracks.[25]

[23] Seddall, H., *Missionary History of Sierra Leone* (London: Hatchard, 1874).
[24] *Imports and Exports for the years 1883 and 1884*;

	1883	1884
Imports	£378,740:19:0	£424,926:18: 9
Exports	£433,633:17:3	£374,821:11:10

This shows an increase of imports in the year 1884 but a decrease of exports in the same year. Culled from *Weekly News*, 21 February 1885.
[25] C.O. 806/266, p. 29.

In a Memorial to the Secretary of State the previous year, the same Association had requested that Sierra Leone traders in tribal areas should be given better protection, that new trading areas should be developed and that, if necessary, force of arms should be used to secure peace among warring tribes.[26]

Though Sir Samuel Lewis's diagnosis was similar, he prescribed a different remedy. He reasoned, according to Hargreaves that:

> The Colony could only prosper if its trade was assured of dependent markets among the interior peoples. Had its settlers been European, this would have been secured long before. Now the attempts to provide security by treaties and stipends having failed, a more active use of military power was needed to suppress tribal war. If this security could be given only by a foreign state, the traders would have to accept it.[27]

In short, Freetown's trading oligarchy sought the reason for their poor trade not in the more widespread economic depression in Europe in the 1880s, but in the discord among their neighbouring tribes. They argued that only an extension of British rule could safeguard their trade and ensure a return to prosperity. This period was also, it must be remembered, a period of imperialism, when nations of Europe were staking their several claims on the African Continent. Thus many factors combined to convince the British Government that British influence in the interior would have to be exercised on a much more formal basis. The results of all these pressures was the establishment of the British Protectorate over the hinterland in 1896.

Governor Cardew, in whose administration the Protectorate was declared, was anxious to develop the territory by building roads, schools and other essential services. For these, capital outlay was required, and Cardew thought that the most realistic way of getting part at least of the funds was to impose a form of direct taxation on the houses in the new areas. The tribal Africans, however, were opposed to the tax, and this, added to their uneasiness about the new order, resulted in a series of uprisings in 1898 throughout the Protectorate, known as the Hut Tax War, during which many European, American and Creole missionaries and Creole traders, the advance guard of western civilization, were killed.

[26] Cf. *Weekly News*, 4 April 1885.

[27] Hargreaves, op. cit., p. 47.

The Creole community in Freetown were aghast at the brutality evinced, and this confirmed them in their worst fears about their neighbours. The Governor, however, accused the Creoles of having advised the Protectorate people to resist the tax, and denounced them in a communication to Joseph Chamberlain, the Secretary of State for the Colonies, as 'Half-educated people who have had free institutions given them which they cannot use aright, and a liberty of the press which has degenerated into licence'.[28] Although Sir David Chalmers, the Royal Commissioner who was sent out to investigate the causes of the disturbances, exonerated the Creoles and blamed instead the policies of the Government, Chamberlain inclined more to the view expressed by the man on the spot, Cardew.[29]

The events of these years are of crucial significance for the subsequent development of the country. It is one of the paradoxes of history that this declaration of the Sierra Leone Protectorate, while uniting the country politically, divided it culturally and ethnically. The new phase actually began with the Protectorate Ordinance itself in 1896 where the policy was laid down that administration of the Protectorate was to be by Europeans. But what was probably the crucial decision had already been taken when J. C. Parkes' plan, drawn up in 1893, for administrating the Protectorate by Creole Agents, was rejected by the Colonial Office on the grounds that it would be impossible to get a sufficient number of qualified Creoles.[30] Thus Cardew, who disliked and mistrusted the Creoles, only extended a line of policy already agreed on. The events of the decade that followed showed the trend of this policy.

In August 1898 an Ordinance was passed which provided for trial by assessors rather than by jury in non-capital cases. The significance of this is the underlying mistrust of the impartiality of the Creoles which was behind the bill, and the deliberate attempt to limit the rôle and influence of the Creoles in the new areas. In 1900, the hated Hut Tax was imposed in the Colony area outside the municipality of Freetown. Further, unofficial representation in the Legislative Council was not increased though this Council was now responsible for the whole of the

[28] C.O. 267/438, Cardew to Chamberlain, 28 May 1898.
[29] Cf. *Chalmers Report* (Parliamentary Papers 1899, vol. LX),
[30] C.O. 267/400, C.O. 267/406 and C.O. 267/407.

Colony and the Protectorate. It was argued that tribal Africans were not ready for this, and that further Creole representation was unacceptable to the Administration. As Hargreaves summed it:

> Leaders of the African bourgeoisie were no longer welcomed as collaborators in the process of improvement from above, and the day of the democratic politician drawing power from below had not yet come. Till it did, the pace of the Colony's progress was regulated by the Protectorate.[31]

Meanwhile, the number of indigenous tribal Africans residing in the settlement had increased, and they tended to settle in particular areas. In the 1890s there were complaints in the local newspapers that the newcomers were creating serious social problems and requests were made for some kind of governmental action. From about 1885, Government had accorded the spokesmen of the respective tribes an unsatisfactory semblance of semi-official recognition, but the position was clarified by the Act of 1905, 'An Ordinance to Promote A System of Administration by Tribal Authority Among the Tribes Settled in Freetown'.[32] This ordinance gave the Governor power to recognize as Tribal Ruler any Headman who with other representatives of the tribe 'endeavours to enforce a system of tribal administration for the well-being of members of the tribe, resident in or temporarily staying in Freetown'. The Tribal Rulers had power to settle disputes between members of the tribe and to collect dues from its members towards the expenses of the administration.

A latent function of this parallel system of administration was that it structured the situation and militated against any rapid integration of the groups in the city; it was unwittingly an attack on the assimilative tendencies inherent in urbanization. The native immigrant in the city had to face two alternatives: he could adapt to the social system of the community in the city or retain his own tribal system. The latter was made easier to accomplish by the policy of the Government in providing a tribal administration system within the city. However, the system has had very little success, as it has failed to command

[31] J. D. Hargreaves, op. cit., p. 97.

[32] A. B. Matthews, *Report on The Tribal Administration in Freetown*, Government Sessional Paper, No. 4, 1940.

the support of the majority of tribal immigrants with western education.[33] Government's policy appears to have been based on the erroneous conviction that the sum of differences between the Creoles and the tribal Africans will always be greater than the sum of their similarities even in the whirlpool of urbanization.

This measure, in conjunction with the changed attitude towards Creole political advancement, was to influence tremendously the subsequent development of Freetown. The process towards acceptance and adoption of Creole culture status was halted at a time when the particularistic policy towards the Creoles had been abandoned.

In actual fact, however, some tribal people were to become assimilated – but only as individuals. A number of them who had to make their living in the town, found it of some advantage to relinquish their social relationships and emotional indentification with their respective tribes and 'pass' as Creoles. This they could only achieve, firstly, if they had acquaintance with western education; secondly, if they posed as church members; and thirdly, if they answered to western or Creole names. All these were rendered easier to accomplish by the anonymity of city life.

These concessions were possible, because the society remained deferential. The tribal groups accepted the axis of subordination/superordination on which life was structured. The Creole subculture throughout the period under review was given positive, while Protectorate or tribal subculture was given negative value. The situation was acceptable to the Creoles because it was not construed as a threat to their ascendancy. Indeed the tribal individuals were the more acceptable because they had come to share the social character of the Creoles.

The acceptance of the Creoles as the desired reference group in Sierra Leone can be variously documented, for example, from the practice of fosterage in the Colony. By this practice, tribal children from the earliest days were put in the care, first of Settlers, and then of Creole guardians who acted as their foster parents. In this way it was expected by the parents that their children would receive education and be introduced to

[33] *Report of the Committee Appointed to Examine the Working of the Tribal Administration (Colony) Ordinance* (Freetown: Government Printing Department, 1955).

the ways of the westerner as seen and interpreted by the Creoles. Many of them were sent to school and profited from the contact. It must, however, be admitted that in a number of cases they were not treated in the same way as bona fide children of the household or afforded the same privileges. 'They are', records the 1931 Census Report, 'useful acquisitions and perform domestic and other work.' No exhaustive study has yet been made of this ward system to warrant any definite statements about the age and numbers involved. It seems, however, from the writer's own knowledge of the situation that the Protectorate children ranged from about six to about fifteen years of age. They helped with the domestic chores in the house which rendered the Creole children free to undertake more leisurely pursuits. Both Banton and Shyllon have referred to these wards in their respective studies though their conclusions seem to differ.[34] Since both were rough sampling surveys, their findings need not be taken as conclusive. The point one wishes to make here is that tribal people accepted the Creole household as a desirable milieu for the socialization of their children and continued to send them to Creole guardians notwithstanding their minor status in these households. The majority of these wards did not return to the Protectorate but remained in the Colony and passed as Creoles; many even took the family name of their respective guardians.

The economic supremacy of the Creoles was next challenged. This was due to a number of factors–adverse trade, change in the policy of the large mercantile houses, influx of Lebanese and Syrian traders in Freetown, and, not least, the policy of successful Creoles themselves in sending their children for professional studies rather than articling them as apprentices in their business. The cumulative effect of all these factors is that Creole participation in the volume of trade–both import and export–decreased.[35]

Political challenge did not come until after the Second World War. It is true that by the turn of the nineteenth century the

[34] M. Banton, op. cit., p. 207.
H. Lynch Shyllon, 'The Effect of the Ward System on Schools in the Colony of Sierra Leone'. Unpublished Dip. Ed. thesis, University of Durham, 1953.
[35] Cf. Annual Blue Books.
N. A. Cox-George, *Report on African Participation in the Commerce of Sierra Leone* (Freetown: Government Printing Department, 1958).

dominant position of the Creoles, though uncontested, had begun to shine with less brilliance and to be questioned by some of their warmest apologists like, for example, Dr Blyden.[36] In a series of articles in the *Weekly News* in 1907, Blyden denounced the Creoles as inferior to the indigenous inhabitants and explained away their catalogue of illustrious men as mere exceptions to an otherwise inexorable degeneracy to which they were all doomed. As Fyfe commented:

> Consigned to failure by their own prophet, the outstanding example of a Europeanized African, soaked in European culture (which, strangely enough, never infected him with the degeneracy he declared his friends could not hope to escape, though he practised none of the native customs he said could alone save them), it was no wonder if they gave themselves up to despair.[37]

But it was not until after the depression which followed the First World War that the economic challenge became sufficiently meaningful to the Creoles to render them aware of their changing rôle in the society. 1870 to 1939 may thus be regarded as the terminal points of the second period of crystallization in the social stratification of Freetown.

[36] H. S. Wilson, 'The Changing Image of the Sierra Leone Colony in the Works of E. W. Blyden.' *Sierra Leone Studies*, N.S., No. 11 (December 1958), pp. 136–48.
[37] C. Fyfe, *A History of Sierra Leone*, p. 619.

Chapter 6

CREOLE SOCIETY AFTER 1939

IN the Second World War and post-war period, the stratification system showed once more the symptoms of status inconsistency. There is a further movement towards a continuum of economic and prestige classes. Schematically, the position can be represented as follows:

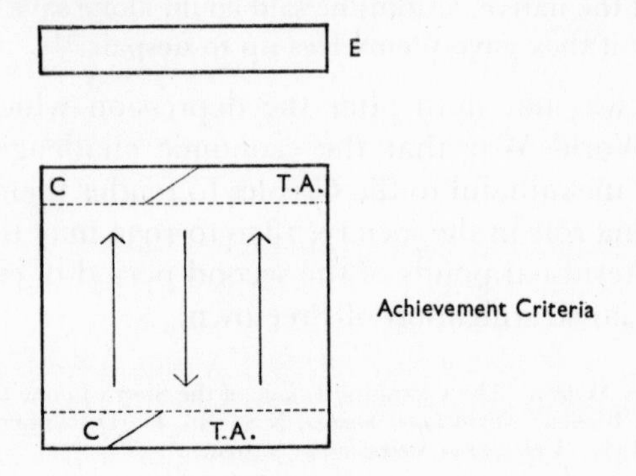

C = Creole: T.A. = Tribal Africans; E = Europeans.

The picture thus suggests an emergent class system based on achievement but with a base largely of tribal people and the old aristocracy at the top though both of a decreasing order. With industrialization and greater participation in the world market economy, it is to be expected that tribal individuals with any amount of education will feel the urge to improve their position. Similarly, the aristocracy who remain at the top will, in the future, do so on the strength of their achievement and as a result of their support of open class institutional norms and not on the basis of any ascriptive premise. In this chapter we shall consider the areas in which Creole monopoly has been challenged and the effects of this challenge on the stratification system.

Until the period of the Second World War, there was no

overt evidence of hostility, resentment or hatred among the majority of tribal people in Freetown because of the structure of tribal/Creole relationship. Both groups accepted the nineteenth century pattern of Creole superiority, mutually recognized social distance, and the deferential behaviour typical of the tribesman towards the Creole. Tribal life, as then structured, did not offer the opportunities for vertical social mobility, and those who were so inclined, had to look outside their society to the urban condition which Freetown afforded.

The motivation behind this mobility striving is many-sided and complex. Banton has given some of the 'push and pull' factors which influenced immigrants in the metropolis.[1] They include curiosity about the source of European power and an attempt to discover that source, flight from tribal taboos and restraints, and, most important, the work incentive. For most jobs, however, a knowledge of English was necessary. And so the tribal individual had to attend the mission or Native Administration school, if he expected any job above that of a labourer in the colony. Economic developments were also generating a change in the consumer requirements of the tribal African. He had to spend more on clothes, as, for example, the wife was no longer content with a new set of *lappa* only once a year. And further, political changes were making it possible for the tribal African, with western education but with no traditional claims to status, to exert some influence in the affairs of his town by contesting a seat in the local district council.[2]

An important factor behind all these material changes was the attitude of the Administration towards the concept of social mobility. In the earliest period the prevailing belief was that there were to be no barriers to the social progress of the Liberated Africans and their descendants in becoming westernized Christian gentlemen. By the 1890s official policy had become modified. The new areas, which the declaration of the Protectorate added, were to be insulated as much as possible from Creole influence and examples. Creoles were no longer the trusted partners of the British in their self-appointed mission of civilization and colonization. The rôles envisaged for

[1] M. Banton, *West African City* (London: Oxford University Press, 1957), p. 132.
[2] P. Garigue, 'Changing Political Leadership in West Africa', *Africa*, vol. XXXIII, No. 1 (January 1953).

them were now the subservient posts in the civil service. The peoples of the interior, on the other hand, were to remain tribal, uncreolized, unsophisticated and unspoilt. It was in this new tradition that a secondary school was opened in Bo in 1906, for sons of chiefs and potential chiefs, and later for others who ordinarily would have gone to Freetown for their education. Announcing the school's formation, the *Royal Gazette* of 29 September 1905, stated:

> Under existing conditions, pupils educated in Freetown almost invariably return home with a feeling of contempt for the native towns and even for their nearest relatives. To prevent this both the native teachers and the pupils will be expected to wear country cloth and their lives outside school hours will be spent in a small town, the government of which will be on ordinary native lines.

Notwithstanding all this, contact between Creoles and tribal peoples in Freetown continued, and each influenced and modified the other. Freetown itself began to look more like any other African city with the increasing preponderance of colourful African costumes. Marriage between Creoles and tribal individuals began to lose its proscription and become a permissive, if not yet a preferred mode of behaviour. An increasing number of persons were to be found who were members of *Porro*, an African secret society, as well as of Freemasonry.

In the middle of the nineteenth century, the Christian community of Freetown had regarded with great disfavour the erection of a mosque in what they felt sure was a Christian city. Today, mosques have sprung up in all quarters of the city and the feast of Eid-ul-Fitri is as much a public holiday and a time of merry-making as the Christian feasts of Christmas and Easter. The degree of syncretism is illustrated by the fact that a recent Mayor of the Freetown Municipal Council, a professed Christian, was made life chairman of the Congo Town Mosque, and at the installation ceremony was named Mohammed Othman Abdallah.[3]

On the other hand, the tribal Africans are being influenced by the culture of the Creoles. As Roy Lewis has written:

> At the very moment when creole culture can no longer expect to be accorded admiration because it is an African adaptation of

[3] *Sierra Leone Daily Mail*, 11 April 1959.

European culture, in fact the attitudes, ambitions and motives of educated tribal Africans and educated creoles are becoming almost indistinguishable. [sic] The educated, literate African, whatever his origins, takes on something of the Creole likeness.[4]

All these have meant a modification or change of the pattern of social stratification in Freetown. With the growth of nationalism, and the opening up of the Protectorate by education and commerce, there emerged a new group of individuals who challenged the ranking order on which the old social structure was based. In turn, there has been a change in the official attitude towards criteria for social mobility. Increasing emphasis is now being placed on equality of opportunity for all members of the society, and tribal Africans are constantly encouraged to improve their social position. It is the acceptance of this universalistic type of institutional norm by the Government (due largely to the diverse factors enumerated above) and the abandonment of the particularistic norm towards Creoles that has created the atmosphere for the present changes. Contemporaneous with these changes, is a shift in the order and significance of the criteria of evaluation. Social ranking is now being based increasingly on occupation, money income and education rather than on kinship and biological descent.

This new class distribution based primarily upon socio-economic factors serves as a basis for social stratification along lines of achieved rather than ascribed status. At the upper rung are the well-to-do class of business and professional men both from Freetown and the provinces often educated in British or American universities; they are generally referred to as the 'senior service'; this class would also include politicians who hold seats in the House of Representatives. The refrain, 'Been to, jaguar, frigful' of the popular Accra song can be taken as indicative of class symbols in Freetown as well.[5]

Another group would include clerks, elementary school teachers and other salaried workers with a secondary but not college education. Then, there would be, in a descending order, the class of semi-skilled workers with very little western education holding some paid jobs in the city. Lastly there are

[4] Roy Lewis, *Sierra Leone* (London: H.M.S.O., 1954), p. 252.

[5] i.e. having been abroad, possessing a car, and being able to entertain in the western manner.

the non-literates who take on domestic employment and other less prestige-giving tasks.

Thus we can conclude that the main basis of evaluation of an individual's status in Freetown is now achievement, not ascription. It is only at the extreme ends of the scale that ascribed status can be regarded as worthy of statistical comment; in the intermediate range, Creole or tribal background is now irrelevant as mechanism for social mobility. This fact that performance criteria are now, in an ever greater measure, taken into account means that the system has changed from a caste-like to an 'open' system to a degree which permits us to speak of social classes in the western sense.

Not surprising or unusual in situations of this kind where the privileged lose their monopoly, many Creoles of the older generation find the changes disturbing. They rationalize their fears in many ways. Some blame the British. They feel they have been let down. They look back to the golden age of Sir Charles MacCarthy and the palmy days of Pope Hennessy when western civilized standards were given highest premium and their ancestors were made to feel themselves the equals of the British. As Roy Lewis observed:

> They had been faithful, in their fashion, to the white men and the white religion; and now they were being thrust on one side. The British were full of the rights of pagans and Muslims. The Protectorate was everything; but who showed the British the importance of the Protectorate–who but the creoles of Freetown? Yet the British did not think the creoles good enough to inherit the land and the power. It was hard to bear.[6]

Others are hesitant and mistrustful about sharing power, not because they believe that leadership from the provinces is now so different or inferior, but because they can see, or imagine they see, behind the line of western trained provincial men with whom they can agree and co-operate, the formidable mass of tribal people with different cultural patterns, amongst whom, some Creoles conclude, they will be swamped, and completely overpowered.

These points of view have implications for the country, two of which are crucial. It has meant, on the one hand, that the

[6] Roy Lewis, op. cit., p. 40.

old pattern of recruiting political leadership from the social élite has been disturbed. Current expectations resemble those which led Count Vergennes to warn his King, as the *Ancien Régime* in France was coming to an end: 'Your Majesty would have to be prepared to see those command who otherwise obey and to see those obey who otherwise command.'[7]

Another consequence of the present situation is that many Creoles who ordinarily would have participated in the public life of the country have withdrawn into their private worlds, a consequence that, in part, accounts for the high proportion of successful Creoles who in the pre-independence period did not wish to return home to appointments but preferred to serve in other countries.[8]

Further, the Creoles had been conditioned to regard themselves as the heirs of the British and the group from which leadership would be drawn. They had been taught, in the tradition of Arnold of Rugby, that in all matters they should become Christian gentlemen. Now they had come to see that the promise of leadership was not going to be fulfilled in that way, and that Christianity was no longer the *sine qua non* for social acceptance. In the circumstances, it is not surprising that behaviour no longer conforms closely to a model social character, but that individuals deviate considerably. Indeed, this is further evidence to support the thesis that the present period is a time of status ambiguity.

In this maelstrom, certain types of personal reactions emerge. There are the extreme reactionaries who wish to uphold the *status quo ante*. They are the 'good old Creoles' who petition the British Government about their inalienable rights and ancestral heritage. There are others, on the other hand, who see the logic of the future and ideologically accept Creole-tribal equality and integration, but whose character structure is not correlated to their thinking. They can reason equality, but cannot feel or act it. Their ideology is, as Fromm would hold, nominal not real.[9]

There is a third group of Creoles who in their collective

[7] Quoted in Laswell, H. D., *et al. The Comparative Study of Elites*. Stanford University Press, 1952.

[8] Cf. Series of Broadcasts by the Africanization Secretary, Sierra Leone, delivered over the S. L. Broadcasting Service, in 1957.

[9] E. Fromm, *Escape from Freedom* (New York: Rinehart, 1941), pp. 277ff.

behaviour attempt to out-Herod Herod in their championship of the cause of the indigenous people. They change to African names, don African robes, advocate polygamy and the inherent virtues of tribal cultures and, in extreme cases, repudiate their Creole ancestry.

There is yet a further type which approximates to the 'liberal reformer' type.[10] Members of this group are ready and willing to work with and for the provinces and believe sincerely that Sierra Leone's future lies in wholeness and integration, not in separateness and conflict.

The events and conditions which are modifying Creole social character have already been mentioned. The existence of these multiple individual character reactions may point to the instability of the times, and may be the gropings towards a third period of crystallization when individual character will conform once more to the character of the society. On the other hand, the present individuation may be only one further evidence of the change in the society towards the urban western type, where as MacIver points out, the individual, as a personality, must make his own terms with society. However, these reactions do indicate that the ethnic-status system in Freetown is in the process of change, that a reappraisal and redefinition of conceptions is being undertaken and that newer patterns are evolving.

[10] Clarence Glick, 'Social Roles and Types in Race Relations' in A. W. Lind, *Race Relations in World Perspective* (Honolulu: University of Hawaii Press, 1955), pp. 239–62.

Part Two

ANALYSIS OF SOCIAL STRATIFICATION

Chapter 7

STRUCTURE OF THE SOCIAL STRATIFICATION SYSTEM

IN Part One an attempt was made to deal with the development of Creole society as a whole historically on a time sequence. Part Two will deal with the processes of social mobility with a closer examination of some of the major indicators of social class position.

More specifically we shall consider how far there has been mutual validation and correlation between Weber's three basic criteria of class, status and power and how far these have been important in determining individuals' life chances and the vertical mobility patterns of the society.

It must, however, be noted that these are not the only factors affecting mobility patterns in Freetown or elsewhere. For example, whenever new positions are created and job opportunities are increased in a society, it means that there are available newer channels by which an individual can become socially mobile.

Or again, class differences in reproduction rates may affect mobility patterns. It was, to illustrate, fashionable, from about the middle of the nineteenth century to about the period of the Second World War, for demographers to argue for an inverse relationship between class and fertility, that the higher the class, the lower the birth rate. The rationale was that in an industrial society, the individual with social and economic ambitions had to make an economic choice, either to economize on children or expenditures; and that by limiting the number of children the individual could more successfully realize his ambitions and retain, if not improve, his social class position. But the upsurge in reproduction rates among the middle classes in Europe in the Second World War and post-war years has necessitated some modification of this prevailing theory of an inverse relationship. It has now been shown that there are other components or factors like attainment of economic security, which can disturb the seeming correlation.[1]

This late nineteenth century formulation of an inverse relationship between class position and fertility was used to explain Creole/Tribal population growths in Freetown. The increase in the influx of non-Creoles into the city was interpreted as positive evidence of the decline of the Creoles. Even Blyden accepted this view and gave it added moral validity by regarding the Creoles as a dying and a degenerate race. Others justified the conclusion by appealing to medical statistics relating to the incidence of diseases. As recently as 1952, Banton in his work accepted as fact the decline of the Creoles and went on to attribute it to social psychological factors: 'that the decline in Creole numbers may be due to, or an aspect of, the decline of Creole influence.'[2]

There are, however, no adequate statistical foundations for this belief in Creole demographic decline. For one thing, from the Census Reports of 1881 and later, the census areas varied from decade to decade, and, throughout, no adequate definition of who and what is embraced by the term Creole was ever made nor was any allowance made for the large emigration of Creoles to the West Indies and other parts of Africa. Thus defective statistics, including birth and death registration, make it impossible to make any reliable pronouncement about the growth or decline of the Creoles. Kuczynski, in his meticulous examination of the census records, has shown that the areas covered by the ten yearly census were not consistently the same; e.g. that the 1871 census covered only the peninsula excluding Quiah, but that it was included in the 1881 and 1891 Census returns; he has also shown that registration returns were not quite complete, and that the probability of error arising out of change or misunderstanding of categories used was common; e.g. some natives in 1931 were returned erroneously as 'Sierra Leoneans'.[3]

In addition to these factors operating in the process of mobility, there is the socio-psychological dimension. How people perceive their chances for mobility affects their movement or stability

[1] Frank W. Notestein, 'Class Differences in Fertility' in Bendix and Lipset, *Class, Status and Power*, p. 272.

[2] Banton, op. cit., p. 102.

[3] Kuczynski, op. cit., p. 281.

almost as much as does the presence or absence of the opportunities. An individual's behaviour and attitudes may be less a function of the class he is in at the moment and much more a function of the class to which he aspires. Thus, both the point of reference and the group of reference often have to be understood, if the sense of a person's class actions are to be understood.

Thus there are two distinct levels of analysis: first the level of the individual in terms of his own adjustment to the society, and second, the analysis of the class structure and its changes.

In short, what it all means is that when an individual changes his position it is firstly because he wants to, however unconsciously; secondly because he is able to change it; and thirdly because the opportunity for change exists. That is, that both the institutional structure and the behaviour patterns of the individuals in a society are equally crucial for stratification analysis.

Chapter 8

PROCESSES OF SOCIAL MOBILITY–STATUS: RELIGIOUS AFFILIATION AND EDUCATION

IN this Chapter we shall consider religious affiliation and education as indicators of status in the Freetown society and as avenues by which an individual or family, properly motivated, can move vertically in the stratification ladder.

Those who were responsible for the Sierra Leone project were not unmindful of the need for some sort of religious organization from the beginning. With the Black Poor in 1787 the philanthropists had sent out a chaplain, Rev. P. Fraser, whose duties included visitations on week days and religious services on Sundays. Clarkson himself acted as his own chaplain until the arrival of Rev. N. Gilbert, the first chaplain appointed by the Sierra Leone Company, who was followed by Rev. Melville Horne in September 1792.[1]

The early attempts at planting missions in Sierra Leone were, however, not very successful. In 1795 the London Baptists sent out Grigg and Rodway, and in the following year, another party arrived in the Colony composed of representatives of many nonconformist denominations.[2] Three days after landing, they all asked to be sent home again, and, with one exception, they sailed for England exactly two months after reaching Sierra Leone. Another unsuccessful attempt was made in 1797. This also was intended to be a co-operative endeavour, but bitter controversy among the members of the mission paralysed the project from the outset.[3]

Religious organization in Freetown did not have to wait for

[1] 'Diary of Lieutenant J. Clarkson R.N.', *Sierra Leone Studies*, vol. VIII, March 1927, pp. 27, 46ff.

[2] They were from the London Missionary Society and the Glasgow and Edinburgh Society. Cf. Lovett, *History of the London Missionary Society* (London, 1899), p. 479.

[3] For these early attempts, cf. C. P. Groves, *The Planting of Christianity in Africa* (London: Lutterworth Press, 1948), vol. I, pp. 208ff.

missionaries from Europe. Many of the Nova Scotian Settlers had been Christians in Canada and on arrival had set up chapels for themselves. The chief, and most important, sections among them were the Methodists, the Countess of Huntingdon's Connexion and the Baptist societies.

These churches were not organizations devoted only to service and worship. They were also centres of social life in the community, providing a field of activity in which the free Negroes could acquire status and exercise leadership. In the early period it was not easy to bring the different religious organizations together into one integrated unit. The church provided an easy opportunity for status enhancement to those with aspirations for leadership. Thus many with great ability and force of personality, if not academic distinction, soon broke away and collected their own following. Mr Thompson, an American missionary, described this process of religious fission as follows:

> One man becomes disaffected and begins for himself, gathering a company around him who are called after his name, then another, and so on. Thus there is Elliott's chapel, Jewett's chapel, this one's chapel, and that one's chapel.[4]

These organizations also reflected the nascent social stratification in the community. In the earliest period the more wealthy and respectable members of the population belonged to the Wesleyan persuasion, mainly because the Nova Scotian Settlers and Maroons were predominantly nonconformists. The rest of the Settler population was in the independent separatist chapels. For example, the chapel of Domingo Jordan served some of the respectable Settlers, while others, like that of the Baptist, Hector Peters, 'had in their train all the lowest of the Nova Scotians'.[5] It was in these less orthodox chapels that there was to be found a display of emotionalism, shouting and shaking which Robert Clarke described as 'an exciting exhibition of finding the Lord'.

[4] G. Thompson, *An Account of the Missionary Labours of George Thompson in Western Africa* (New York, 1852). For analysis of church leadership as a ladder of advancement in other societies, cf. B. Sundkler, *Bantu Prophets in South Africa*, 2nd edition (London: Oxford University Press, 1961). F. Frazier, *The Negro in the United States* (New York: Macmillan, 1949).

[5] Rev. S. A. Walker, *The Church of England Mission in Sierra Leone* (London, 1845), pp. 147 ff.

Thus the Liberated Africans had to face a people who had accepted church going and membership of a religious group as part of their way of life; an acceptance aided by the Government and the missionary agencies, as these all believed in the civilizing influences of the Christian religion. Little time was lost, however, in absorbing the newcomers into the Christian faith.

At first the nonconformist sects were the most influential. But their position was to be successfully challenged, partly because of their tendency towards fission and partly by the foundation in 1799 of the Society for the Spread of the Gospel to Africa and the East, which became known as the Church Missionary Society. The most serious example of this tendency towards fission occurred in 1844 when the Settlers refused the Liberated Africans the use of the 'big pulpit' in their Rawdon Street chapel. As a result many of the Liberated Africans left the society, taking with them some chapels in which they had influence and leaving Rawdon Street chapel as an exclusively Settler place of worship.[6]

The reasons for the success of the Church Missionary Society are not far to seek. For one thing, it was, in some ways, an offshoot of the old Sierra Leone Company; for the leading members of the latter, like Thornton and Macaulay, were among the founders of the society. It was thus privileged from the beginning. Secondly, unlike the nonconformists, it adhered to the doctrines and practices of the Established Church of England, and thus enjoyed official patronage and support.[7] As a result, its prestige was enhanced considerably, so that by the middle of the century, it had become the most prestigeful of the denominations.

[6] 'The building situate at the corner of Westmoreland and Waterloo Street in this city, was erected in the year 1850 at a cost of about £1,500 by the united efforts of the Liberated Africans and their descendants who had been denied religious equality among the Methodist Settlers of Rawdon Street Chapel, from whom they seceded a few years previously.

'The name "Samaria" has a deep meaning attached to it. The despised few when they first met to give a name to their new church, argued long over it, until a brother with some degree of warmth rose and said, "Let it be called SAMARIA 'for the Jews'–referring to the Methodist Settlers evidently–'have no dealings with the Samaritans'."' *Artisan*, No. 7, vol. III, 14 July 1888, p. 3. Also cf. C. O. 267/218.

[7] 'The Society has already four settlements on the coast of Africa, in which 200 native children receive Christian instruction. These settlements are subject to the caprice of the natives; but the institutions in question will be secure under the protection of the Colonial Government of Sierra Leone.' *15th Annual Report of the C.M.S.*

The periodic influx of newly arrived Liberated Africans into the Freetown community, where the Settlers had already set a standard based on western ideas, had confronted the Government with a major social problem. It was strongly felt that through education and religion the Liberated Africans could be brought within the pale of civilization, and, to this end, an appeal was made to the C.M.S.[8]

In 1816 an arrangement was effected between the Colonial Government and the C.M.S. by which the latter undertook responsibility for the welfare and religious instruction of the Liberated Africans and for the management of the Colonial Church in Freetown.[9] The C.M.S. became responsible for staffing the Liberated African villages with ministers and schoolmasters, the Government agreeing to subsidize them.

The Church of England, through the C.M.S., thus became the denomination of officialdom in the colony. The process was begun by which recaptives were made 'children of God and inheritors of the Kingdom of Heaven'. Some missionaries insisted on individual conversion prior to baptism but some administrators, like Governor MacCarthy, urged a more liberal policy which would allow general baptism of all adults, converted or not.[10] As they were thus ushered into the new western society, so they were given European names in place of their tribal ones, which were regarded as heathenish. The C.M.S. invited their subscribers to suggest names for their wards;[11] but many Liberated Africans preferred the names of secular personalities like Nicol, Coker, Macfoy, and adopted them accordingly. Many, however, did not abandon completely their African names. Thus there developed the practice which is still observed, of giving a child a European as well as an African forename, the one for use in contact with Europeans and western institutions, the other now referred to as 'ose'

[8] 'I felt persuaded that by their being placed under respectable clergymen devoted to a life of privations in the cause of humanity their wants would be better attended to and they would in the course of a few years be made useful members of the community by receiving an education suitable to their probable situation in life.' MacCarthy to Bathurst, 31 May 1815, C.O. 267/41.

[9] S. A. Walker, op. cit.

[10] C.M.S. Archives, London. *Journal of W. A. B. Johnson*, CA1/E7/47.

[11] 'It is proposed to receive into this Institution the multitude of African children who are liberated from smuggling slave vessels. Any benevolent person who gives five pounds per annum may have the honour to support and educate one child, and may affix to the child any name he pleases.' *The Missionary Register*, June 1815.

name for the more intimate contact with the family and other kinsfolk.

The religious bodies in this Christian *rite de passage* were acting, albeit unconsciously, as agents of British expansion and colonization. No doubt, to the missionary, baptism was the new birth by which the individual was made a child of Christ and an inheritor of the Kingdom of Heaven. But by the giving of his new name, the Liberated African was also ushered into the western type of society that was emerging. In fact, Governor MacCarthy looked upon baptism as 'an act of civilization'.[12]

Typical of the early missionaries was the German, Wilhelm Bernard Johnson, who came to the colony in 1816 and died on a sea voyage to England in 1823. He was the statesman, priest and administrator of the people in his mountain-valley village of Regent in the Parish of St Charles. Missionary agents like Johnson were responsible for both the material and spiritual welfare of their parishioners. They acted as magistrates, supervisors of schools, Government superintendents, priest and clerk, all in one. Johnson, we are told, was responsible for distributing rations twice a week to the Liberated Africans.[13] All aspects of community life seemed to have been centred around the church. For example, on 27 December 1821, at a meeting of communicants, a law had been framed by themselves, that if any person should start a quarrel or behave as did not become a Christian, he should be turned out and fined five shillings or be confined in the House of Correction for two months.[14]

In 1859 the C.M.S. and Wesleyan societies were joined by the Roman Catholic Mission. Its beginnings were humble. True to the teachings of Ignatius Loyola, it concentrated in the early years on free education in its own schools and on the young. In 1866 the Sisters of St Joseph of Cluny arrived in Freetown and established a convent school. Growth was slow, and Freetown was for long their only centre. But in the 1890s a foothold

[12] *Journal of W. A. B. Johnson*, p. 94.
'Of this I am certain that religion and civilization which as the necessary consequence of religion is but another name for it, must effect here, what they have uniformly wrought in every other part of the world, a concomitant improvement in arts and science and a correspondent elevation of the human character and race.' Macarthy to Bathurst, C.O. 267/41.

[13] The rations consisted mainly of rice and some oil and salt. Cf. *Parliamentary Papers*, vol. XI, 1842.

[14] Seddal, *Missionary History of Sierra Leone* (London: Hartchard, 1874), p. 193.

A. T. Porter (1834–1908)

was acquired in Sherbro, and in course of time, stations were opened in the interior.[15]

The small independent sects faced strong competition from these more formal organized churches which had outside assistance, both in terms of money and personnel. The latter came to be associated with the white race and, therefore, with progress. Thus Africans who sought social prestige, political power, and economic security were not content to remain in the smaller or independent sects unless they had obtained leadership in them.

At the top of the ladder of preferment was St George's Cathedral, the diocesan seat of the Anglican church. Then came the other Anglican churches and the more formal Wesleyan chapels. Some of the smaller independent churches had begun to amalgamate; for example, the Baptist and the Church of God.[16] Others were closing down or being swallowed up. Many families were moving, as their material position improved, from a smaller to a larger church, from independent chapels to mission churches and from the Wesleyan to the Cathedral.

The history of Arthur Thomas Porter, contractor and hotel-proprietor, will illustrate this process. The Freetown newspaper, *The Weekly News* of 2 September 1893, described Mr Porter as 'a native of Sierra Leone of Maroon and West Indian extraction'. His father, Guy Porter, was at one time Manager of the Liberated African village of Kent.[17] In the 1850s, Arthur Porter worked as a mason in the building of Samaria Church. In the

[15] In 1913, only 3,250 Catholics were reported in a population of about 1½ million. Cf. Latourette, *History of the Expansion of Christianity* (London 1947), vol. v, p. 456.

[16] F. Butt Thompson, *Sierra Leone in History and Tradition* (London: Witherby, 1926).

[17] Guy Porter, a West Indian, was Manager of Kent 1831, gaoler, Freetown 1833. Governor Macdonald replying to charges against him in connexion with Porter's wife, wrote that Porter had been a servant in England, was for a while gaoler but now kept a common eating house. C.O. 267/194 10 November 1846. Macdonald in reply to Ex-Governor Findlay.

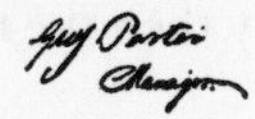

The above is a photograph of his signature on the Census return in 1831 when he was Manager of Kent, cf. C.O. 267/111. Crown copyright; reproduced by permission of the Controller of H.M. Stationery Office.

paper, *Artisan*, for 8 August 1885, he is listed as one of a number of successful businessmen who started life as an artisan. In 1889 he paid his first visit to England, during which time he was initiated as a freemason on 18 July in Richmond Lodge No. 1011 E.C. in Manchester. He was at that time a member and trustee of the Wesleyan Maroon chapel. In 1892 he opened a hotel which he called 'Porter's Royal Hotel'. *The Weekly News* of 18 December 1893 carries an advertisement of the facilities of the hotel which included 'excellent cuisine, wine at moderate prices, Bass' ale and stout on draught, billiard room and bar, large airy bedrooms'. The assistant manageress was a European lady, Miss Nellie Farrell. But in the same paper, *The Weekly News*, two years later, in the issue of 7 December 1895, Arthur Porter is now among Cathedral members signing an address to Bishop Ingham. His obituary in 1908 referred to him as 'an ardent churchman and Treasurer of the Native Pastorate Church'. This movement from nonconformism to the more prestigeful denomination, the Anglican, can be documented from the history of several other families now prominent in Anglicanism.

The chief task and opportunity of religious organizations in the early period had been one of capturing the support of the motley crowds who found themselves within a new social setting. With success, went the building of large places of worship, the employment of a specialized and full-time ministry and the increasing acceptance of general cultural standards as practical definition of religious obligation.

It was the desire of the C.M.S. to make the church in Sierra Leone self-supporting and served by its own clergy. Partly to this end, in 1827, it founded the institution, Fourah Bay College. The Society also pressed for the creation of a bishopric which was achieved in 1852. In 1861 the C.M.S. withdrew their European missionaries, and the work was taken over by the Africans themselves, the church becoming the 'Native Pastorate Church'. In 1875 the Colonial Government withdrew its subsidies to the Church, but by then the roots were already securely planted.

It must also be noted that the desire for religion on the part of the Liberated African matched the proselytizing zeal of the Government, the missions and the Settlers themselves. Many

Liberated Africans, realizing the need for adaptation to the new order of the Settler and the white man, turned to the church and the missionaries because of the social and economic advantages that would accrue from such affiliation and because of a desire for guidance in making the necessary adjustment to the new environment of Freetown.

It is of some significance that there was no organized resistance on the part of the Liberated Africans to the Christian religion. As Forbes tells us: 'One of the ruling passions of the Liberated African is to become a member of some civilized religion'.[18]

It is suggested that this non-resistance–indeed this passion–was due, among other things, to the pattern of church affiliation already set by the Nova Scotians and Maroons. But the fact that these Liberated Africans found themselves in Freetown without support of their own cultural milieu may have caused a feeling of insecurity and instability. When, therefore, they came in contact with the Christian religion they were eager to embrace it, for it supplied a new consciousness of group membership which otherwise would have been lacking.

Material success of the Liberated Africans meant that the C.M.S. had a core membership of rising citizens. So the Anglican church grew in wealth and importance. In it the social climber was also able to make the necessary contacts, while his membership of it in turn enhanced his own social position. The church reinforced the position of people who already enjoyed economic security.

As on the question of names, the Liberated Africans and their descendants succeeded in incorporating into their new religion more specifically African practices which commemorated important events in the life cycle. Thus, whatever the denominational differences, certain rites were regarded by all as indispensable, such as circumcision, baptism, marriage and the rites of death. A denial of these signified not only a defection in worldly prestige, but also a threat to eternal well being. Circumcision was widely practised, though, as the evidence suggests, it was not copied from the Nova Scotians.[19] Nor is it likely that the practice was derived from their recent introduction to

[18] Forbes, *Six Months in the African Blockade* (London, 1849), p. 12.
[19] *Artisan*, 19 March 1887.

Hebrew religion. It seems more plausible that the basis was their own African custom in Yoruba and Ibo land–a custom prevalent in many other parts of Africa, as was substantiated by the similar rite among the Mende and Temne of Sierra Leone, modified only to the extent that, in the latter cases, it was performed on adolescents, not infants.

Though common law living was practised, it was invariably the ambition to convert it at some later stage, into a more formal kind of union in church. And not to be able to provide a decent funeral, which meant a church funeral, for a dead relative, was regarded by the Liberated African as an unpardonable insult to the dead, and a confession of abject poverty by the living relatives. Further, the dead were regarded as a continuing influence for good or evil, on the lives of their descendants, and must on no account, therefore, have withheld from them those ceremonies that were associated with prestige and grace.

By the last decade of the nineteenth century, the tendency towards separation, which had characterized the early period, reappeared. In the early period, fission was an indication of the need for satisfaction and fulfilment which only came from positions of leadership. The separatist churches of this latter phase, however, did not command a large following nor did they represent the rising or more influential members of the community. The principal concern of these sects, unlike the more formal institutionalized denominations, was with adult membership. There was in addition a high degree of congregational participation in the services and administration of the group, unlike the delegation of responsibility found in the denominations. Another marked dissimilarity is the racial orientation of the sects. These are wholly African, and are indifferent, if not openly hostile, to the prevailing aspirational patterns. The two most important sects in Freetown are the Church of Martha Davies Confidential Band and The Church of the Lord (Aladura).

Throughout the nineteenth century, the Church flourished among the Settlers and Liberated Africans and their descendants. It was, as we have noted, more than an attestation of faith; it was also indicative of successful adjustment to the westernized social setting that had emerged. It served as one evidence separating those who had arrived from the rest. The Christians had made the grade; others were the 'unto whom', referring to the Biblical quotation 'Unto whom I swear in my wrath that they shall never enter into my rest'. As Banton testified: 'On two occasions I inadvertently asked Creoles to what tribe they belonged and received the answer, "I am a Christian".'[20]

The church also served as an important training ground for leadership and forensic skill. Ezzidio, the first African to be nominated into the Legislative Council in 1863, was a devoted Methodist local preacher. And Wilhelm Grant who followed Ezzidio into the Legislative Council in 1869 had learnt the rudiments of committee work, which made him a useful member of the Council, as a member of the Native Pastorate Church Committee. It is also of significance that weekly class and prayer meetings, a characteristic feature of nonconformism, were taken over by the Anglican communion in Sierra Leone, and many had their first training in organization as leaders of their respective class meetings. Thus the Church also served as an ideal training ground for the secular rôles of the future.

Today, church affiliation as an indicator of class position is on the decline. The work of evangelization is still carried on in Freetown but with the emphasis now on the immigrants. In April 1960, a survey of Student Opinions and Attitudes at Fourah Bay College on matters of public interest was carried out by the members of the Social Science Seminar which the writer conducted by means of a questionnaire. Of a student population of 326 of whom 178 were Sierra Leoneans, 146 Nigerians, 2 Ghanaians, answers were received from 204 students in the following categories.

Students born in Sierra Leone	89
Students born in Nigeria	100
Other African countries	2
Not identifiable from the filled-in questionnaire	13

These were all students pursuing degree courses in the faculties of Arts, Science and Economics and in the postgraduate diploma in Education course. To a question requesting the students to assess the relative importance for stratification of five criteria

[20] H. Banton, op. cit., p. 109.

viz. descent, wealth, education, occupation and religion, none of the Sierra Leoneans gave the first choice to religion while sixty-three of the eighty-nine, that is, about seventy-one per cent. of the Sierra Leoneans placed it at the bottom of the scale. On the other hand fifty-two per cent. rated education as the most important.[21]

Many factors will account for this change. Firstly, it is in general keeping with the modern trend towards greater secularization of society. As Roy Lewis wrote:

> Once it was sufficient to be a good Christian; that would unlock all the doors and make a man equal in stature to any other man. Now the West appears a great deal less earnest about Christianity, and ready with a dozen new and conflicting explanations of the whole duty of man, black or white.[22]

Secondly, many have developed new interests outside the field of religion. The European official class and the 'been-tos' set the fashion of driving to beaches or playing tennis or just lazing around the house on a Sunday morning. Watching a game of tennis or football in an afternoon is now infinitely preferred to attending choir practice. Religion is now at most a secondary criterion in determining position in the system of social stratification.

Complementary to religion was education in furthering the accommodation, first, of Liberated Africans and then of the tribal people into the social setting of Freetown. Indeed, religion and education are almost inseparable, for the school developed, not as an institution in itself, but as a function of the church. In fact, it can be said that, until quite recent times, wherever

[21] The question reads as follows: How important in your country today are the following things in deciding to which class a person belongs? Place the number 1 opposite the criterion you think the most important, 2 opposite the next and so on.

	1st	2nd	3rd	4th	5th	No Answer
	In percentages					
Who his family is	10	10	18	47	8	7
How much money he has	19	28	28	12	7	6
What sort of education he has	52	27	6	11	2	2
What job he holds	18	28	31	16	3	4
What his religion is (i.e. Christian, Moslem, Pagan)	–	4	10	7	71	8

My thanks are due to the Bureau of Social Science Research Inc., Washington, D.C., for working out the IBM tabulations and codifications.

[22] Roy Lewis, op. cit., p. 40.

there was a church building, there was a school attached to it: the building was used for worship on Sundays and for inculcating the new learning on weekdays. The church was thus the channel and the interpreter of western ideals and values as, many centuries before, it had been the means of introducing Graeco-Roman culture into northern Europe.

Because of the humanitarian background to the foundation of the colony, it is not surprising that there were schools almost from the arrival of the first Settlers. Education was regarded as an important avenue by which the blessings of civilization would permeate through Africa. In commenting on the fourth quarterly examination of the scholars of the Colonial School, the *Sierra Leone Gazette* for 3 January 1818 records:

> It is from the foundation of education that we must expect the stream of civilization to flow; it is that which enlarges the mind, and thus renders it capable of every other improvement.

The earliest educational effort in the colony was the work of Rev. Patrick Frazer, the chaplain who had accompanied the Black Poor in 1787. In 1794 the Sierra Leone Company sent two schoolmasters, Jones and Garvin, to take charge of their school for the Settler children.[23] And from 1804 we find the Church Missionary Society, and from 1811 the Wesleyan Society, contributing powerfully to educational work in the colony.

When, after 1807, Liberated Africans began to be admitted into the colony, some arrangements were made for their education in the villages which were created for them. In addition, there was a Female Captured Negroes School in Freetown itself until 1816.[24] In 1817 there were in Freetown apart from the denominational schools, a 'Daily Colonial School for Boys', 'Daily Colonial School for Girls', an 'Evening Colonial School for Boys' and a 'Sunday Colonial School for Girls'. Apparently these were only for Settler children.[25] In that same year, these schools came under the C.M.S. as part of the arrangements of 1816 already referred to. In 1840 there were, according to Mr Miller, Inspector of Schools:

[23] C.O. 270/2, Regulations for Schools approved at a Meeting of Council, January 1794.

[24] C.O. 267/43, Rules to be observed in the Female Captured Negro School.

[25] C.O. 267/45.

Forty-two schools, of which 14 were schools of Government, 6 of them being instituted for and receiving exclusively Liberated African children, while 8 are formed as exclusively of children, born in the Colony. The remaining 28 are conducted by the Church Mission, or by the Mission of Wesleyan Methodists, and receive Colony born Children only.[26]

Commenting on the different types of schools, Miller wrote:

In a colony expressly founded among other objects for the removal of all those exclusive ideas and hateful distinctions of caste which have been fostered by slavery, the best means that could be adopted are in this way used to renew and maintain them. The Creole children receive rapidly those ideas of their own superiority to which all are so prone. The young Liberated Africans, who have been emancipated from the greatest degradation and misery found themselves still humbled in their own esteem and that of others as an inferior race. These distinctions are further encouraged by the Apprenticeship system and they are continued through life.[27]

Clarke, Senior Assistant Surgeon to the Colony of Sierra Leone, made similar comments when he wrote about the 1830s that:

The Creoles are taught in schools separate from the Liberated African children. This distinction inspires the Creole children with ideas of their own superiority, which they discover on every occasion; and to such an extent is this feeling fostered, that I have often heard the Creole boy or girl when they quarrelled with one of the Liberated African children, call them niggers, which is to the latter the most opprobrious of all opprobrious epithets. This separation, then, of the Creole from the Liberated African children, has not only tended to depress and stupify the latter, but has given the former unjustifiable ideas of superiority so much so that the two classes will not associate.[28]

Miller recommended, among other things, that there should be an admixture of Colony and Liberated Africans in the schools; but, he warned, that each school must have a fair representation of Creoles, never that 'excess, namely, of barbarism over civilization – the leaven of the latter becoming insufficient to leaven the entire mass'.[29]

[26] C.O. 267/166. Enclosure in letter from Doherty, 27.10.1841.
[27] Ibid.
[28] R. Clarke, *Sierra Leone Customs and Manners* (London, 1843), p. 33.
[29] C.O. 267/166. Enclosure in letter from Doherty, 27.10.1841.

Charlotte Village School *circa* 1885

By permission of the Colonial Office

Governor Fergusson, in his comments on the educational system, accounted for the separation in terms of wealth and the prestige it conveyed. He wrote:

The Government schools were opened to all classes but the Creole population preferred paying for education under the European teachers of the Missionary Society, to the gratuitous teaching of native teachers in the Liberated African schools, and thus was the separation rendered complete.[30]

Even about the time these words were penned, the Liberated African had begun to make that progress in the economic order which in time was to affect his status ranking.

By the 1840s it was becoming clear that some educational institution to meet the requirements of the more successful Liberated Africans and Settlers would soon be a necessity. Governor Macdonald expressed similar sentiments when he wrote in the Blue Book for 1841–2:

A school for boys is much required. . . . The want of an establishment of this description to which the better class of the inhabitants might have an opportunity of sending their children is much felt; at present they must either be content with a very low standard of education, or must put themselves to the very great expense of sending them to England, an expense which but very few indeed could bear.[31]

This type of education was achieved in 1845 when the C.M.S. (now Sierra Leone) Grammar School was founded. A few years later, in 1849, a similar institution was founded for girls. These schools were intended for families with sufficient wealth to pay for the training of their children in certain class rôles.[32]

Education in these schools was to be of a superior kind to that of the ordinary schools. It was in these schools that the children

[30] C.O. 267/189. Fergusson 94, 26.11.1845.

[31] C.O. 269/176. Macdonald 78, 24.11.1842.

[32] Cf. Letter from C.M.S. House, 26 June 1850 to Herman Merivale relating to schooling for illegitimate children of Europeans. ' . . . in establishing a superior Female School for a select number of pupils, who all pay for their education, and who will probably become the wives of our ministers and teachers, it was judged that the native females born in lawful wedlock had a prior claim upon the resource of a religious society. Also that the conceding to them this priority would tend to uphold the honour of marriage in the estimation of the community, and counteract a too prevalent notion in all such societies that the native female is honoured rather than disgraced by illicit connexion with Europeans.' C.O. 267/218.

of the old Settler groups who had been able to maintain their social position and the children of the Liberated Africans who were becoming successful in trade were united in a common set of social standards and practices.

Education was thus, in Freetown, one of the important mechanisms providing for social mobility. It was, and still is, part of the royal road to success and to positions of power and prestige.

The children of successful Liberated Africans comprised the majority of the pupils in the Grammar School. This was in part evidence of the material and social progress which the Liberated Africans had made and the corresponding stagnation if not decline of the Settlers.

As the Governor testified in the 1840s:

> The successful prosecution of a petty trade, combined with the steady observance of great temperance and economy in living have in the course of years raised many of this body to a state of comparative affluence.[33]

Descendants of Settlers and Liberated Africans were soon to be found in the registers of the Grammar School, the C.M.S. Female institution, known as The Annie Walsh Memorial School, and the Wesleyan Boys' High School, founded in 1874 to give a similar type of education. For example, in 1852 we find A. B. C. Sibthorpe, a Liberated African descendant, and A. T. Porter of Settler parentage, being admitted into the Grammar School on the same day.

Education thus ushered the individual into the world of western civilization, literature and technology. To the Liberated African this was quite different from his own background. Thus, in various ways, the school taught the child new rôles for participating in the emergent western society.

Until about the beginning of the twentieth century, no sustained attempt had been made to bring the tribal immigrant into the orbit of the Freetown society. Thus Ingham could write in his book, *Sierra Leone After A Hundred Years*:

> Every school, whether elementary or high, as we pass them by is quite full, and yet the streets swarm with children, for there is no such thing as compulsory education. And all about us, sitting down

[33] C.O. 267/175. Fergusson, 12, 30.1.1842.

and eyeing our possessions, taking a job when they can get one, at other times stealing, are these country people, who are coming amongst us in such increasing numbers, and for whom there is as yet no adequate provision. If it be asked, to what extent do the older residents mix with these people? the answer is, that the latter form a class for the most part below them. They are their servants. Illicit connection there may be, but not intermarriage. Sometimes a large party of superior-looking natives will arrive in the town from the interior countries, whose object is an interview with the Governor. They sit down in some quarter, keep to themselves, have their interview and return. It is very much the same with those who come to trade.[34]

True, a number of tribal youths, as isolates and not in the mass, had received formal education in the colony schools.[35] It is also true that the type of education did not really prepare the students for maximum appreciation of life in Africa. But these are not for the present our immediate concern. The point is that this kind of education which gave prestige, imperfect though it was, was not pressed for by the tribal immigrants or their spokesmen in the nineteenth century. The *Poro* Society for boys and the *Sande* for girls had given the tribal individual the kind of education he or she required for living in a tribal society. But a knowledge of basic English soon became a necessity for successful living in Freetown. In addition, the affairs of the Colony were conducted in English and, therefore, some form of literacy in the language was essential for almost any type of clerkship. The parallel was drawn by A. B. C. Sibthorpe in his history of Sierra Leone where he referred to the Grammar School as the 'Sierra Leone boy's porroh bush'.[36]

In time, the Protectorate accepted this fact of the necessity for literacy in English, and pushed for the education of her sons.

[34] Ingham, *Sierra Leone After A Hundred Years* (London: Seeley, 1894), p. 290.

[35] For example, the fourteen foundation members of the Grammar School included five boys from Gallinas and one from Port Lokko in the Sierra Leone interior. Cf. *Historical Sketch of the Sierra Leone Grammar School* by A. E. Tuboku Metzger, 1935, p. 8. And we read in 1860 of the S. L. Government supporting three sons of native chiefs at the School, cf. C.O. 270/23.

[36] Quoted in Tuboku Metzger, op. cit., p. 55. Porroh (sometimes spelt 'poro') is a male secret society institution among a number of tribes in the rain-belt of Africa. Boys and youths spend from three days to a month in the enclosure, called the 'bush', during which time they undergo initiation rites and are trained to take their place as adults in the tribal society. The female institution is known as 'Sande' or 'Bundo'. Cf. Kenneth L. Little, *The Mende of Sierra Leone* (London: Kegan Paul, 1951), pp. 240–53.

The indigenous Africans were no longer content to leave their children with Creole families for training; many were now stipulating a condition that the children must be sent to school.

In 1906 Bo School was founded by the Government to provide western education for the sons and nominees of Paramount Chiefs. A year later, the Albert Academy was founded in Freetown by the Evangelical United Brethren (headquarters in Ohio, U.S.A.) where boys from the provinces were taught together with Creoles. In 1925 the Government founded its own boys' secondary school in Freetown, i.e. the Prince of Wales School.

All these developments have meant that opportunity for education is now more broadly available. Children with either the necessary fees or scholarships and with the required scholastic attainment can now enter any of the secondary schools. This does not mean, however, that these are the only determining factors. Other variables like attitude towards education in general or towards different schools in particular, aspirations for social mobility, also affect the number who actually want to go to school. However, the point can now be made that whereas in the nineteenth century the opportunities for education were unevenly distributed, the present trend is for the education systems to be open to those who can pay the fees and are qualified to enter or who gain scholarships, irrespective of ethnic background. And the present Government has promised free primary education in a few years' time. Thus the education system underscores the change that is taking place in Freetown from a particularistic to an open-universalistic type of society.

Education also acts as a bond which overrides ethnic distinctions. 'An educated individual visiting another town as a stranger can always be sure of hospitality in the home of other educated people' writes Kenneth Little.[37]

Religious affiliation and education are thus indicators of status and of the mechanisms by which individuals rise or fall in the social stratification system of Freetown.

[37] K. L. Little, 'Structural Change in the Sierra Leone Protectorate', *Africa*, vol. xxv, No. 3 (July 1955), p. 225.

Chapter 9

PROCESSES OF SOCIAL MOBILITY–STATUS: 'SYMBOLIC JUSTIFICATION'

'IN all societies', writes Barber, 'men's acts and possessions have at least three different functions: the instrumental function, the aesthetic function, and the function of symbolizing their various social rôles and position.'[1] In this chapter we are concerned with activities and possessions insofar as they are indicative of social class position. These symbols do not occur as single and isolated units, but in clusters, which can be regarded as the 'style of life' appropriate to the respective class. Components of a 'style of life' will include recreational and eating habits, residential area, style of dress and such like. The type of house and its location within the community can, in conjunction with these other symbols, indicate social class position of an individual or family in the society. Thus, London's West End or Boston's Beacon Hill symbolize upper class position, though not only upper class people now live in those areas.[2]

In Freetown the area which carried greatest social distinction in the nineteenth century was the area around the landing-place of the Black Poor and the first settlement of the Nova Scotians. This area became known as Settler Town. When the Maroons arrived in 1800 they were located west of the Settler settlement, and their area was soon known as Maroon Town. Similarly, when lands further west of the Maroon settlement were reserved for the Kroo population in the colony in 1816, that area was known as Kroo Town. As the Kroo men were mainly deck hands on board ships, the area they occupied took on a low social connotation.

The style of house which the Settlers erected, with its stone foundation and wooden superstructure, seemed to have been copied from the colonial architecture of the New World they

[1] B. Barber, op. cit., p. 136.

[2] Walter Firey, *Land use in Central Boston* (Cambridge: Harvard University Press, 1947).

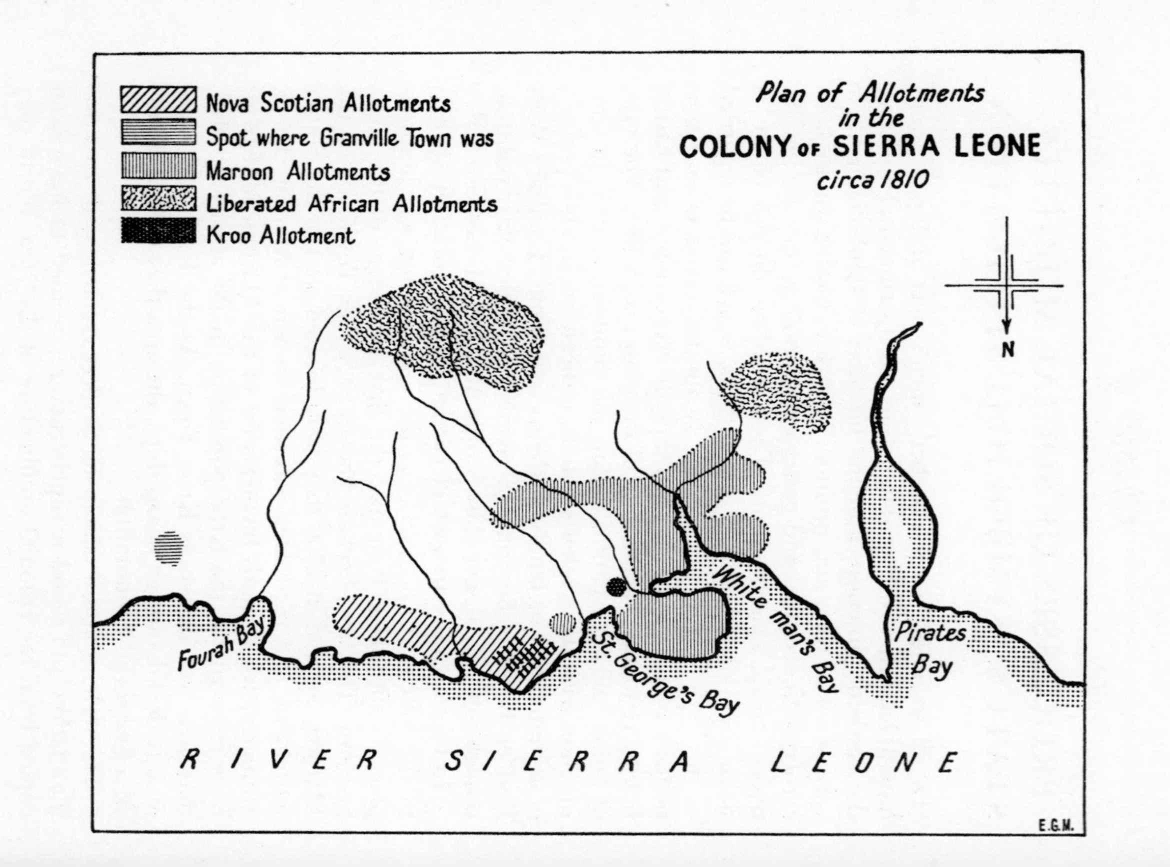
Plan of Allotments
in the
COLONY of SIERRA LEONE
circa 1810
Nova Scotian Allotments
Spot where Granville Town was
Maroon Allotments
Liberated African Allotments
Kroo Allotment
N
Fourah Bay
St. George's Bay
White man's Bay
Pirates Bay
RIVER SIERRA LEONE
E.G.M.

had known. Settler Town also contained the main Government buildings, the stores and the larger houses.

Governor Fergusson, in his description of Freetown in 1839, showed that with the periodic addition of Liberated Africans and the material progress of a number of the latter, the society had become more elaborately stratified. At the bottom were the most recently arrived Liberated Africans who, like the tribal immigrants, lived in mud houses. Next were the petty traders and the skilled workers like tailors, masons and carpenters who occupied frame houses. Above these were the more successful who lived in frame houses reared on a stone foundation of from six to ten feet in height. About these houses, Fergusson wrote:

> They are painted outside and in; have piazzas in front and rear, and many of them all round; a considerable sprinkling of mahogany furniture of European workmanship is to be found in them; several books are to be seen lying about, chiefly of a religious character; and a general air of domestic comfort pervades the whole, which, perhaps more than anything else, bears evidence of the advanced state of intelligence at which they have arrived.[3]

Fergusson continued,

> Persons of the highest grade occupy comfortable two-storey stone houses, enclosed all round with spacious piazzas. These houses are their own property, and are built from the proceeds of their own industry. In several of them are to be seen mahogany chairs, tables, sofas, and four-post bedsteads, pierglasses, floor-cloths, and other articles indicative of domestic comfort and accumulating wealth.[4]

We have already mentioned the Act of 20 August 1853 confirming the Ordinance No. 6 of June 1852 which conferred the rights of natural born British subjects on the Liberated Africans. One of the main reasons for the bill was to remove all doubts as to the rights of the Liberated Africans to hold land and property within the colony.

Thus location and type of dwelling contributed to status ranking. A house built on the frame house pattern carried more prestige value than a mud house of the circular type which had characterized tribal African architecture. An analogous situation had occurred, as Labat found in the Gambia in the eighteenth century, where the *casa a portuguesa*, a rectangular

[3] W. Fergusson, *A Letter to Thomas Fowell Buxton, Esq.* (London 1839), p. 9.
[4] Ibid., p. 11.

shaped house, had come to be preferred to the more traditional circular house by those who could afford to build new houses.[5]

Dr Poole, writing about the Colony in the mid-nineteenth century, noted this preference for the western style of housing including the fireplace and other paraphernalia. He wrote:

> Many of the houses are very good, substantial and commodious and much attention has of late been given to the construction of the buildings in style and material. The stores or shops are on the ground floor in general, and the rooms above these are used for domestic purposes. The kitchens are, invariably, distinct from the dwelling in some part of the yard; most of them are airy and spacious, well furnished and English in every respect. The principal dwellings are well aired, and lighted by glass windows, supplied with fire-places, and displaying all the necessaries and knick-knacks essential to complete an English parlour and drawing room. The floors are matted or covered with oilcloth, and sometimes carpeted: the walls are tastily papered and ornamented with paintings and prints. Gay chandeliers, suspended from the ceiling, light up the dinner table on grand occasions. The easy chair, the ottoman and the sofa are there; and mirrors and looking-glasses to enliven the apartment and gratify the vanity.[6]

Until the end of the nineteenth century, there were no particular areas reserved for the English population in the city. However, by the beginning of the twentieth, it was decided that owing to the difficulty of making the whole of Freetown free from malaria, it would be more feasible to drain a small area and keep it under control. Thus, Hill Station to the west of Freetown was chosen as the site for this experiment and was turned into a reservation for the European population, which from then on was no longer housed in houses rented from the Liberated Africans in Freetown. In this way, geographical distance was translated into social distance, and the resulting decrease in income arising from the loss of the European house rents contributed to Creole economic decline.[7]

Since the European population was on the average better

[5] J. Labat, *Voyage du Chavalier des Marchais en Guinée, fait en 1725, 1726 and 1727* (Paris, 1730), vol. 1, p. 161.

[6] T. E. Poole, *Life, Scenery and Customs in Sierra Leone*, 2 vols. (London: 1850), vol. 1, p. 93.

[7] '. . . a mountain railway has been constructed, and a cantonment built on the hills, thus permitting of the Europeans residing in the hills and of their segregation from infected natives.' *Sierra Leone, Medical Report 1905*, p. 7.

paid, better educated and occupied better houses than the majority of the African population, and since they unquestionably practised that way of life which had been reinterpreted by the Creoles, their removal to the western suburbs of Freetown conferred a new social distinction to that part of the city. It soon began to rival the central area of the city as the dwelling area of the more socially mobile of the population. It became increasingly fashionable to live outside the city municipal boundaries on the western side. The feeder villages to the east of the city did not, however, confer the same distinction.

With the political and other changes consequent on the Second World War, the exclusive reservation of Hill Station for whites only was modified, and residences were provided for heads of Government departments irrespective of race or colour. Thus, Dr E. A. Renner, an African and late Director of Medical Services, had his home at Hill Station, and the ministerial quarters for political ministers are situated at Wilberforce Spur, the area adjacent to Hill Station. The intervening area between Hill Station and municipal Freetown, that is to say, Wilberforce, Signall Hill, Wilkinson Road and Spur Road, are the areas which now carry the highest sale price per town lot of all areas in the colony. For instance, while land outside the strictly commercial sites can be obtained for about £30 per lot, land at Spur Road is now being offered at about £150 a lot.

This trend in symbolic justification towards the bigger and western designed type of houses is now a recognized channel by which those who feel they have 'arrived' try to validate and justify their new position. Thus the preference, where the material means can bear the cost, for cement blocks rather than mud, for rectangular rather than circular, houses is shared by both Creoles and the tribal immigrants. In all this, it must, however, be stressed that housing or residential area alone does not establish true class position. Social class indentification is a process that takes several symbolic indications into account.

Another indicator which contributes to the indentification of status position in most societies is the style and quality of clothing. In classical China, for example, the upper-class Mandarin symbolized his class position by his long gown; he also wore his fingernails long as an indication that he did not perform any manual tasks.

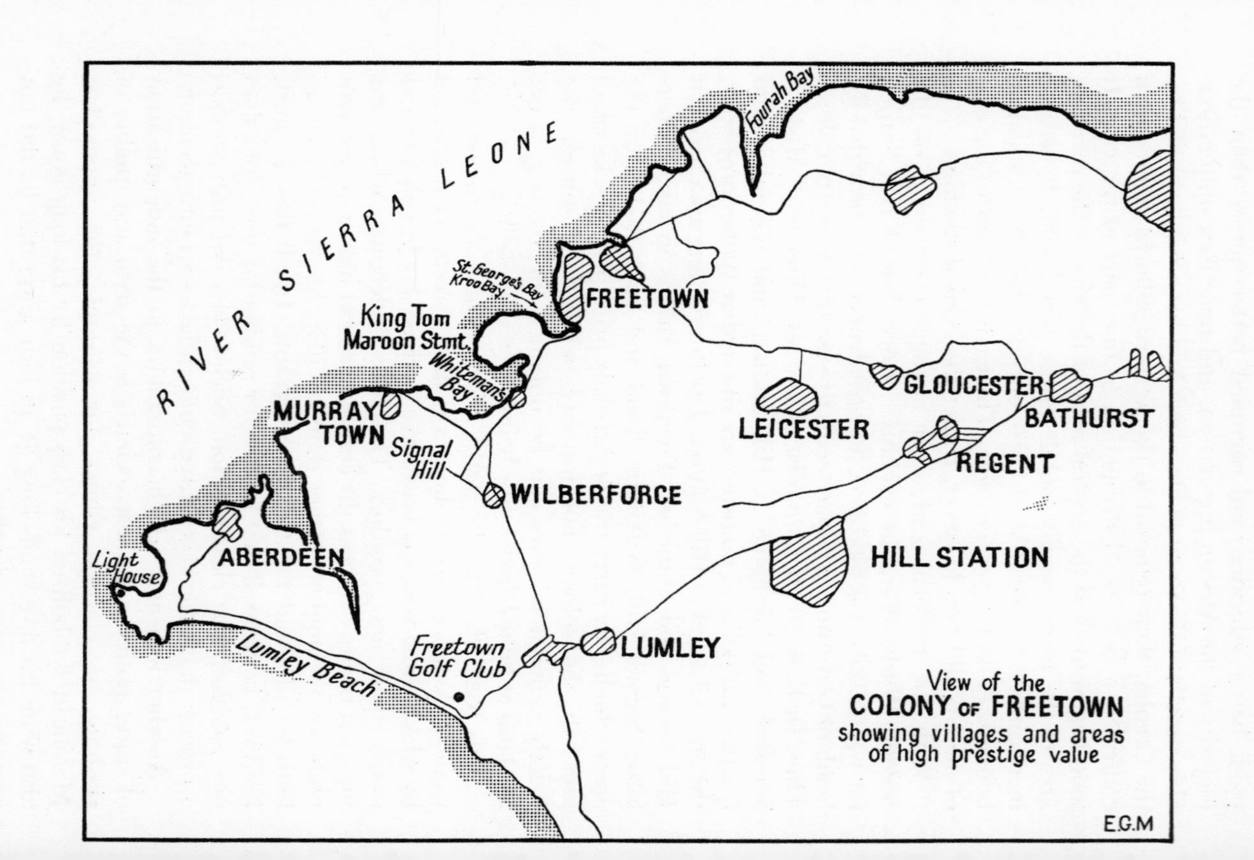

View of the
COLONY OF FREETOWN
showing villages and areas
of high prestige value

In Freetown, from its earliest days, it was noticed that the form of dress was one of the differences separating the indigenous inhabitants or the tribal individuals who drifted into the settlement from the Settler from the New World. In the 1890s a Dress Reform Society was started to persuade young men to wear African traditional dress. But it did not succeed. Indeed, instead of gowns replacing coats and trousers, 'Muslims came to wear trousers under their gowns, and their wives to copy the Christians' tight-lacing and feathered hats.'[8] Today, while differences in attire are still perceptible, they are not so obviously correlated with ethnic descent when comparing individuals in more or less similar income brackets.

As has already been noted, Freetown afforded the Liberated African his first contact, outside the slave ship, with western culture. At the start these Liberated Africans had no use for European clothes and found the food and the cooking abhorrent. Clarke reports how they used to tear up the clothing given to them on landing.[9] To encourage them further, and so reduce the gap between the Settlers and themselves a proclamation was issued in 1834 requesting conformity on the part of the Liberated Africans to the European dress of the Nova Scotians and Maroons. Section 111 of the Proclamation read:

> And whereas large sums of money have been expanded by the British Government, and many valuable lives sacrificed, in rescuing these Liberated Africans from perpetual slavery, who are now enjoying in the Colony, all the benefits and blessings of freedom, and as their gratitude for such benevolence cannot be better testified than by conforming, according to their respective circumstances in life, to the rules, customs and manners of British subjects. It is hereby further ordered and declared that all Managers of Districts and Justices of the Peace within the Colony aforesaid, shall, in future, strictly prohibit all Liberated Africans under their superintendence or observation, from assuming any other dress than that usually adopted by Europeans.[10]

Kenneth Macaulay, the businessman of the firm of Macaulay and Babington and cousin of Zachary Macaulay, had referred to the Settler Society of those days as a 'black aristocracy,

[8] C. Fyfe, *A History of Sierra Leone*, op. cit., p. 468.
[9] Clarke, *Sierra Leone Customs and Manners*, p. 181.
[10] C.O. 267/119. Enclosure in Findlay 2.3.1833.

embued with European tastes and habits, and with a proper sense of the decorum and decencies of civilized life'.[11] In 1845, the principal inhabitants of the colony petitioned the Governor and Council that a similar proclamation respecting dress be ordered for all inhabitants in the colony, aiming this time at the tribal immigrants. This petition was prompted, they alleged, because of the 'indecent scenes of nudity hourly witnessed in our streets'.[12]

However, the position must have improved, for ten years later, Rev. S. W. Koelle was able to write:

> In most parts of Africa clothes are far too sparingly used to answer the requisites of propriety. In some countries the women cover themselves only with leaves, or a handful of twigs, and in others both sexes live in a state of absolute nudity. In Sierra Leone the people are decently dressed – in the church, on Sunday, cleanly and prettily. Some negro gentlemen and ladies even appear in silks and satins; and the practice of women going about with their bosoms uncovered becomes rarer every year.[13]

Mrs Melville made similar observation about Freetown around 1849. She wrote:

> The settlers in the colony, and also the slaves that have been emancipated here, who are termed 'liberated Africans' assimilate their dress to that of Europeans; the wealthier sort wearing jackets, waistcoats and trousers of cloth, white duck or blue baft, with broad-brimmed straw hats tied round with black or coloured ribbon, or round smart cloth caps, while the ordinary apparel of domestic servants consists of a white jacket, check shirt and duck trousers.[14]

Thus the western type of dress served the newcomers into the community as symbols of prestige. It became one of the strong indicators of the degree of assimilation which had taken place. 'Petticoats and trousers' was one way of aspiring by action to membership of the desired culture status. The Liberated African abandoned the scanty attire of slave status or the dress of his tribe and adopted the western garb. The Victorian notions of respectability and preference for dark and sober colours came to dominate in Freetown.[15] Men preferred

[11] C.O. 270/22. [12] Ibid.

[13] S. W. Koelle, 'A Picture of Sierra Leone in the Light of Christianity', *C. M. Intelligence*, 1855, p. 51.

[14] Melville, *A Residence at Sierra Leone*, ed. Hon. Mrs Horton (London: John Murray, 1849), p. 21.

[15] Cf. Meade's definition of a 'civilized blackman' – 'he dresses in the European fashion and can sit down to table and eat clean'. C.O. 267/328.

woollen suits to cotton, and top hats and spats were a common feature in the Freetown streets, especially on a Sunday morning. Indeed, Alldridge, writing about Sierra Leone around 1900 tells us that the top hat was then the emblem of paramount chieftaincy, such had been the extent of its influence.[16] This picture carries us towards the end of the nineteenth century. Today the top hat is rarely seen, though Lewis feels that many Creoles would welcome its return.[17]

With the increasing knowledge in the twentieth century about proper attire for the tropics, and the manufacture of clothes specifically for use in warm climates, the European population which, in the final analysis also influences the fashion of the day, now dress more lightly and more simply. The open-neck shirt now rivals the semi-stiff collar except on more formal occasions, and a pair of shorts is as popular as trousers for day-to-day work.

The younger elements among the Creoles soon came to similar conclusions; so while their fathers dressed and sweated in woollen suits, their sons dressed in lighter textures or were unencumbered by tie or jacket. Thus when the tribal individual in the 1920s began to challenge Creole ascendancy in the economic order, he tried also to justify and validate his material or economic success by enjoying that 'style of life' which had traditionally characterized the Creole class. They entered the race, however, at a stage when the Creoles had abandoned the top hat and coat for the khaki shorts and shirt. The new groups aim to join the ranks of the Europeans and the Creoles not only as wielders of economic and political power but also as a standard-setting group in the sphere. Hence, as Dr Busia pointed out about an analogous situation in Ghana, the new groups aspire, depending on their economic success, to bigger cars, more expensive clothing, larger houses and more items of conspicuous consumption than either the European or well-to-do Creole could ever afford.[18]

One other indicator of social position in this context is the type of food consumed and the ritual governing the serving and eating of food. Perhaps one of the most significant practices

[16] T. J. Alldridge, *A Transformed Colony* (London: Seeley, 1910), p. 271.
[17] Roy Lewis, op. cit., p. 5.
[18] K. A. Busia, 'Gold Coast Elites', *Inst. Soc. Science Bull.*, No. 3, 1956.

which Creoles have propagated is that of assembling in public and mixing with persons other than one's own kin group for purely social and recreational purposes. In traditional tribal culture, for example, people only go out of their houses or meet in public for some fairly specific reason, and once the business is over, they disperse.

Here again, as in the matter of dress, greater emphasis was given on the whole to European fare, though it was on this symbol, food, more than any other, that the Liberated Africans were to be most successful in influencing the habits of the Settlers. This is not surprising since food is one of the most conservative areas and usually one of the last to be affected when an individual accepts elements from alien cultures. Typical dishes of the Creoles now include jollof rice and foofoo and palaver sauce–dishes which in their preparation and serving are hybrid and show the influence of both the New World and the old Africa.[19]

As has been noted, the Settlers on arrival were maintained by a supply of provisions and stores from England because they were unaccustomed to the native fare around them. Provisions included beef, pork, biscuits and cheese, oatmeal, barley and butter.[20] This kind of food was more akin to that of the European administrative class than to that of the indigenous Africans in their midst, and so helped to underscore social distance and enhance the prestige of European fare. But there was never a sufficiency of the English foodstuffs on which the community could survive without some addition of the local food.

Rice, however, became the staple food of the Settlers as it

[19] Essay on Foofoo by J.S.T.D.

'In Abeokuta and the Aku-speaking countries, Cassada was formerly a fence-plant; i.e. a plant used for marking boundaries, and was used as food only for slaves and cattle. . . . When the Aku man was brought as a slave from the interior and sold to the Spaniards and Portuguese on the Coast he found in the slave barracoons at Lagos, not foofoo, but manioc, cassava, or as it is called at Lagos "Garri". Liberated in Sierra Leone he met fields of cassada. . . . He longed for something that would look in its starchy mass like his *dombai*. He grated his cassada. . . . Its kind had never been seen in their country, and so they had no name to call it by. But it was *so white* when grated that they–the Akus–called it *fu-fun*, white or the white food. The name "Foofoo" is well known in the West Indies, and signifies any pounded or boiled edible mass, whether made from plaintain, cassada or yam. But it is evidently a name borrowed from Sierra Leone. . . . At any rate it is not found in "Webster's Unabridged" as it was very likely to be, if it was a Tropical American word.' *Artisan* No. 12, vol. III. Saturday 22 September 1888. Alternatively, 'Fufu' is an Ashanti word brought to Freetown by the Maroons.

[20] Clarkson's Diary, quoted in Ingham, op. cit., p. 91.

had been in the period before their arrival.[21] In the preparation of dishes such as the ground-nut chop or the jollof rice they were influenced very much by the West Indies and the Gambia. The Liberated Africans were to add some of their own dishes–particularly the palaver sauce–to those of the Settlers as part of the culinary heritage of the Creoles. About the eating habits of the Liberated Africans, in the 1830s, Clarke had this to say:

> The universal custom amongst the Liberated Africans, is to eat soon after getting up. Akarah, Chappulah, Aggedi, or perhaps a portion of some fruit as pineapple, banana, etc., according to the taste of the individual, are the articles usually taken. Breakfast is eaten about half past ten or eleven o'clock, a.m., . . . Their favourite dish is called Palaver Sauce.[22]

A further evidence of the influence of the Liberated Africans on the resultant Creole way of life is the popularity of their feast, the 'Awoojoh'. This is a feast which is held on special occasions as, for example, before a marriage or after a death or at any time when it is deemed necessary to bring the whole family together–both the living and the dead–in some ceremonial partaking of food. The Settlers had a similar feast, called 'Bamchu', which is now only rarely observed. It can be suggested that the primary reason for the disuse of the *bamchu* is that it is basically the *awoojoh* transformed under new world conditions. *Bamchu* begins at dusk and ends, passover-like, before dawn, the type of food consumed being predominantly western – tea, bread and butter, cakes, hog's head soup, and some alcohol. *Awoojoh* is celebrated during the day and consists of a meal of African foodstuffs, such as bean cakes fried in palm oil, fried plantains and palm wine. It is suggested that the Negroes under conditions of slavery could not afford a day off from work to celebrate the feast of *awoojoh*; thus they could only gather for the feast at night, and, in the circumstances, ate the kind of food they could get in the southern states of the United States of America. By the same reasoning, it was easier for Settlers and their descendants to revert, under the influence of the Liberated Africans, to the *awoojoh*, since that was the feast their parents

[21] 'Rice is the principal food of the natives although they have cassada, yams, eddies, sweet potatoes, and great varieties of other roots and vegetables unknown in Europe.' Matthew, *Voyage to the River Sierra Leone* (London: 1788), p. 57.

[22] Clarke, op. cit., p. 54.

had intended to celebrate under the changed conditions of the New World.[23]

Throughout the late nineteenth century there was an increase in the western influence on Creole cooking. In the 1920s, wrote Butt-Thompson:

> On a fire in the open, with utensils almost elementary, the servants will prepare roast yams and serve them mashed with a butter and egg sauce and much seasoning; or fritter bananas or plantains or oranges, in a fashion that would do credit to a chef, and to the real satisfaction of those visitors who have grown tired of salted meat and canned vegetables.[24]

In contemporary Freetown, the ground-nut stew and the jollof rice, the custom of inviting non-relatives to a meal for no specific religious or ceremonial reason, are now symbols of socio-economic groups rather than of Creole/tribal differences. As further example, there is in Freetown the Junior Dinner Club which is made up of the European professional and commercial men and their opposite numbers in the Creole community and the educated élite from the provinces. They meet once a month for dinner and friendly discussion. The dress for the occasion is western–a dinner jacket or tuxedo–and the food is always some variation of English/Creole cuisine.

Another aspect of status is the changing pattern of race relations in the Colony and its significance for the stratification structure. For the most part of the nineteenth century race patterns were by and large cordial. A number of the early Church Missionary Society clergymen, like Nyländer, Wenzel, and Renner, and traders like Broadhurst and George Nicol, had married Nova Scotian women. Equally, Creoles, like Michael Jarrett who qualified as a doctor in the 1870s, and J. B. M'Carthy who qualified as a barrister, married English girls and brought them out to join Freetown society. Some dispensed with the formalities of marriage. Sir Charles MacCarthy, for example, found solace with Hannah Hayes, daughter of an African mother by a European trader, by whom he had two children. And illegitimate children of mixed unions

[23] A. T. Porter, 'Religious Affiliation in Freetown, Sierra Leone', *Africa* (Jan. 1953), vol. XXIII, No. 1.

[24] Butt-Thompson, *Sierra Leone in History and Tradition* (London; Whitesby, 1926), p. 259.

THE 'SENIOR SERVICE' IN 1885, *showing its inter-racial composition*

By permission of the Colonial Office

were able to rise in the occupational structure. Thus, Charles Heddle, the prosperous ground-nut trader and member of the old Governor's Council from 1845 until its dissolution in 1863, had an African mother. So had John Meheux who from 1855 until his death in 1886 was Sheriff of the Colony.[25]

There were, however, some who did not regard the practice of miscegenation with the degree of approval and enthusiasm which Portuguese and Brazilian writers like Texeira da Mota and Gilberto Freyre now tend to accord it. Governor Kennedy's confidential Despatch of 1 August 1853, gives some glimpse of a degree of intimacy between the races in the country which might not have been extensive but which seemed highly concentrated. He wrote:

> The confusion, cabals, heart burnings arising from illegitimacy are indescribable. The following outline which I believe to be strictly according to fact may illustrate the subject. I will omit names, having no desire to do more than justify the foregoing remarks. Mr A, an officer in one of the courts is the illegitimate son of the former judge of the court by a black woman. Mr B, his junior in the same office is legitimately born of a white woman by the same father. Mr A is married to an illegitimate daughter of Mr C (a white man) of a black woman. Mr C was a member of the Legislative Council. . . . Mr D in the Secretary's office is the illegitimate son of the new judge in the Colony by a coloured woman. . . . Mr D is married to the illegitimate daughter of Mr E (later a magistrate and member of Council) by a black woman which woman is now married to one of the most wealthy and intelligent of the coloured men of the Colony. . . .[26]

There was not in those days, as there was from the early twentieth century, any area cleared and reserved for the European population; they lived in the town, often in houses rented from the Africans and as neighbours. There were mixed

[25] C. H. Fyfe 'The Administration in 1885', *Sierra Leone Studies*, N.S., No. 4, June 1955, p. 227.

[26] Cf. 267/233 Kennedy, 1 August 1833. The following is suggested as key to the abbreviations:
A=William Smith, official of the mixed court, son of a European judge and a Fanti woman.
B=Frederick Smith, clerk of the mixed court, William's white half-brother.
C=Kenneth Macaulay, Zachary Macaulay's second cousin.
D=Walter Lewis, Secretariat Clerk.
E=Benjamin Campbell.
Wealthy and intelligent coloured man=W. H. Pratt.

social clubs and an integrated administrative service. It must be admitted that the European population in those days was small, and contiguity plus the absence of white female company of any number, contributed to the atmosphere of cordiality.

The conclusion drawn from this review is that the symbolic indicators of status position which, in the early period of the colony, correlated to a large extent with ethnic descent, today are broadly components of socio-economic groups. This reinforces the conclusion that except for the extreme polarities, the differences which divide people in Sierra Leone are increasingly those which are based on the extent and success of the process of industrialization and westernization achieved by the individual. In the past the Creoles, by making use of the opportunities provided, were able to achieve and monopolize the prestigeful positions. Now that these opportunities are being extended to include all, the early advantages of the Creoles are being gradually overcome.

It must, however, be emphasized again that these symbols are not always true or scientific indicators of class position or that the corollary always holds that people in a certain class position will always exhibit certain symbols. However, though symbolic indicators are only a clue to social class position and need further validation, yet they do show that the basis of stratification in Freetown is changing from a particularistic oriented to a universalistic type.

Chapter 10

PROCESSES OF SOCIAL MOBILITY–CLASS: OCCUPATION AND WEALTH

IN the Freetown context, as in most societies, the economic criterion in terms of occupation and wealth has been a crucial index of class position and a determining influence in the transformation of the society and of the individual as he moves vertically or horizontally in the stratification structure. It was initially through wealth that the Liberated Africans entered the world of the Settlers. They achieved economic parity with the Settlers before gaining social acceptance or sharing political power.

The first Settlers to arrive in Freetown, as has been recorded, were the Black Poor from England. These, it would be recalled, were either former domestic servants or disbanded soldiers, and it was their lack of any economically productive skills and the fear, among other things, that they might increase London's social problem that induced the Committee under Hanway to plead their cause with the British Government and to organize the first settlement.

Granville Sharp, however, soon found the project unwieldy for one individual or on the basis of philanthropy alone; and so he joined forces in 1790 with a number of trading men to form the St George's Bay Company, which was changed into the Sierra Leone Company in the following year. From then on the trading interest became predominant in the affairs of the Colony.

From 1791 to 1807, Freetown was governed by the Sierra Leone Company, and the system of administration which they had devised was taken over almost unaltered when the Colony passed under the Crown on 1 January 1808. The leading members of the Sierra Leone Company then, i.e. after 1807, formed themselves into the African Institution whose object was to promote the civilization of Africa and to keep a watching eye over the Colony of Sierra Leone.[1] The Secretary of this committee was Zachary Macaulay who had served as Governor of the Colony under company rule from 1794 to 1799. With a Colonial Secretary knowing little and caring less about Sierra Leone, the African Institution was instrumental in not only advising on the policy to be pursued but also in the selection of European personnel for service in the administration of the Colony.

As was to be expected of the mercantile class, the Sierra Leone Company hoped to introduce legitimate commerce in place of the traffic in slaves which had characterized the West African trade. And, partly to this end, English firms established commercial houses from the earliest period, an example of which was the firm of Macaulay and Babington. Their merchandise included 'cotton goods of various quality, pots, shoes, braces, knives, spoons, hinges, bill books, smoothing irons, sealing wax and pencils'.[2]

From 1815 onwards, it was customary to have a member representing the mercantile interest sitting in the Governor's Council.[3] The influence of the trading class had become so entrenched that it was possible in 1835 for the Council to agree to a motion not to pass any legislation (presumably legislation of a financial nature) which came before it, without the interest of the merchants being first taken into account.

This enviable position of the trading class was further reinforced by the failure of the Liberated Africans to convert their barren plots of land in the villages that were formed for them into successful agricultural holdings.[4] Many, therefore, began to take up residence in Freetown, either as peddlers, porters or boatmen.[5] Others began to venture inland or to make contacts

[1] Viscountess Knutsford, *Life and Letters of Zachary Macaulay* (London, 1900), p. 281.

[2] C.O. 267/56. This despatch also includes a list of trading merchants in the Colony in 1822.

[3] N. A. Cox-George, 'Financial System of a West African Colony in relation to Economic Development' (unpublished Ph.D. thesis, London University, 1954), p. 4.

[4] Notwithstanding William Allen's efforts in encouraging agriculture and farming. He was instrumental in sending casks of cotton seeds for the use of the Africans. C.O. 267/78. Allen, 11.7.1826.

[5] Another reason has also been adduced, viz. that the farms were abandoned because of fear of native risings; that the Liberated African preferred the security of the city. Cf. *Papers Relating to the State of West Coast Settlements*. C.O. 267/29. This could hardly explain the movement away from the mountain villages which were

with tribal settlements along the rivers, mainly for the purposes of trade or barter.[6]

In consequence of both these sets of factors – the proprietary and trading origins of the colony and the success attendant upon trade – the mercantile occupation became the predominant in the sense of the most prestigeful of occupations throughout the greater part of the nineteenth century.

In the retail trade, the Liberated Africans were able to outstrip the Settlers primarily because their needs were fewer and they were thus able to plough back a greater proportion of their profits into their enterprises. It was also comparatively easy for the Liberated Africans to compete with the Europeans, for from the 1830s the only European traders in the Colony were private individuals trading on commission from London houses, and not companies with more fluid capital.

Another contributing factor in the success of the Liberated African can be traced to the influence of Protestantism. Max Weber has asserted that modern industrial capitalism could not have emerged without the 'inner-worldly ascetism' which contributed to the personality formation of the entrepreneurial middle class, the groups in which capitalism had its origins.[7] A similar hypothesis can be utilized to explain Liberated African success. It can be argued that the Liberated Africans were able to triumph over the second generation and less puritanic Settler competitors because of their attitude to their work as fostered by the evangelical religion. Their occupation became a calling to which Providence had summoned them, and thrift, saving, honesty and assiduous toil became virtues recognized as directly enjoined by their religion.

In the Liberated African villages around Freetown, the main occupation was agriculture in the mountain districts, and fishing in the seaside villages. A precarious living was eked out by planting and selling garden products like lettuce and tomatoes in the one instance or by catching fish and selling to the people in Freetown. Gradually an increasing number began to move

free from native risings. Indeed, by the time the Liberated Africans landed, fears of native risings (i.e. Temne) had subsided.

[6] 'Multitudes of them are yearly passing from the condition of predial labourers to that of petty traders and artisans.' C.O. 267/172.

[7] Max Weber, *The Protestant Ethic and the Spirit of Capitalism*, trans. T. Parsons (London: Allen and Unwin, 1930).

into the neighbourhood of Freetown, looking for work with a greater renumeration than the villages could yield. The first occupation they went into was that of hawkers; they sold in the streets a number of cooked edible substances, prepared according to recipes they had known in their country of birth, such as 'agidi', 'abala' and 'akara'.

Next they moved into the petty trade in the market, selling articles such as nails, fish-hooks, door-hinges, ribbons and needles. Many also bought wholesale goods brought by canoe down the rivers from the interior which they retailed at a profit. Those who had been apprenticed were able to work as tailors, cobblers, blacksmiths, carpenters, masons and such like. By the 1850s many had succeeded in owning their own canoes which plied the rivers in search of products to sell in the Freetown market, while others owned small shops. 'At sales of prize goods, public auctions, and every other place affording a probability of cheap bargains', wrote Governor Fergusson to Fowell Buxton in 1839, 'they are to be seen in great numbers, where they club together in numbers of from three to six, seven or more to purchase large lots or unbroken bales.'

In the retail business the Liberated Africans were able to undersell and compete successfully against the Europeans for the same reasons as they had outstripped the Settlers; that is, by dint of hard work, frugal living and fewer overhead costs. Many of this grade were able to realize considerable sums of money, and some even chartered ships which carried their products to England and brought back English goods for their stores and some even owned the vessels which carried their coastal trade. For example, Shreeve mentioned the purchase of a Schooner by Daniel Coker for £300, and William Faulkner, a Liberated African had bought a prize ship for a similar amount in 1839.[8]

Forbes, writing a little later, had this to say:

> The Liberated African often rises into a man of property, and eight or ten thousand pounds is by no means an uncommon sum for them to possess. On dashing steed, they may be seen galloping round the race course in the evenings. Two in particular, Messrs. Pratt and Isidore, are men of great wealth, and merchants in the colony.[9]

[8] Shreeve, op. cit., p. 31.
[9] Forbes, *Six Months' Service in the African Blockade* (London: 1849), p. 13.

And there was also Peter Newland, a Liberated African merchant, who died in 1846 leaving an estate in houses, merchandise and cash of upward of fifteen hundred pounds. And there were many others – John Ezzidio, W. H. Pratt, John Taylor, Thomas Carew. These men rose to positions of power and prestige predominantly on the basis of their success in trade.

In the 1870s Freetown was a prosperous trading community. Commented the *Church Missionary Intelligence* for April 1877:

> The Sierra Leone man is a connecting link between the European trader and the uncivilized tribes in the interior. It would be strange indeed if he did not avail himself of this peculiar advantage, and employ his energies in a direction affording so much scope for them.[10]

In this way, the energies of the rising African middle class were diverted from politics to commerce because of the favourable conditions for individual enterprise.

These successful merchants, in order more fully to validate their social position, endeavoured to give their children that component of upper class status which they had missed, viz. a sound western education and preferably admittance into one of the learned professions. Thus, their sons, instead of being apprenticed into their several businesses, were sent to England to study a profession – principally law and medicine. As, for example, Abraham Spencer Hebron, who was sent to Monkton Coombe School in England by his father, Abraham Hebron, a wealthy rum merchant of Kissy Road, and later to the Inner Temple where he was called in 1882, and subsequently became an Honourable member of the Legislative Council in Freetown in 1898. By the last quarter of the century these professions had begun to take the place of pre-eminence which trading had occupied. In the 1890s Sierra Leonean medical officers, sons of prosperous merchants, whose fathers had borne the expenses of their training included Dr William Renner, who had studied in London and Brussels; Dr M. L. Jarrett, who had also studied in London and was an L.R.C.P. of Edinburgh; and John Farrell Easmon, M.D., and his brother Albert Easmon.[11] Lawyers, trained in England, included Samuel Lewis, Claude

[10] *C. M. Intelligence*, April 1877, p. 23.

[11] M. C. F. Easmon, 'Sierra Leone Doctors,' *Sierra Leone Studies*, N.S., No. 6, June 1956, pp. 81 ff.

Wright, Montagu Thompson, T. J. Thompson, J. Shorunkeh Sawyerr–all sons of successful merchants.

The rise of a professional class corresponded with the decline of commerce among the Creoles. This decline was in part caused by the lack of adequate personnel with the zeal and drive of the entrepreneur which had characterized the merchant-owners. Those sons who returned to their fathers' businesses, came back largely because they had failed to qualify for one or other of the professions. It is not too surprising, therefore, that in the hands of these sons, business declined.

Another factor contributing to the decline, and in some ways a resultant of the decline, was the increasing participation of the Lebanese and Syrian traders in the retail trade of the country. There is no conclusive evidence for dating exactly the beginning of Lebanese and Syrian penetration into West Africa. Marwan Hanna, who has done some research on this, believes that immigration into Sierra Leone must have taken place sometime in the late 1880s.[12] However, they were of sufficient numbers and had gained an appreciable portion of the retail trade of the country to make them the target for Creole outbursts during the risings in 1919 following the First World War.[13]

While the dwindling Creole merchants kept to the beaten tracks established by their entrepreneur fathers, the Lebanese and Syrian traders ventured further inland, selling cheap textiles and other articles the Africans might need and buying in return the local produce which they sold to the European exporting firms in Freetown. Soon they were able to build up a credit worthiness with the European banking firms, and credit facilities were offered to them on a scale higher than was extended to their African confrères. In these ways, the Lebanese traders were able to extend their range of retail goods and their buying activities, and thus they attained their present position of a near-monopoly of the trade between the predominantly wholesale operations of the European commercial houses and the petty trade of the African.

[12] Marwan Hanna, 'The Lebanese in West Africa: How and When They Came,' *West Africa*, 26 April 1958, p. 393.

[13] 'They have succeeded in establishing themselves as traders in the Colony as well as in the Protectorate and to their success in this direction is to be attributed in no small degree the engendering in the minds of a certain section of the African community of a jealousy which led to the Anti-Syrian riots in 1919.' *Sierra Leone Census Report, 1921*, p. 10.

Another reason for Creole business decline was that around the 1890s the European firms began to engage in retail trade thereby depriving the Sierra Leone trader of one sure source of profit. As Alldridge noticed in his book, *A Transformed Colony*:

> The whole system of trade has undergone an entire revolution. Formerly the large European firms were merchants pure and simple, in the old fashioned sense of the term. That is to say their business then was strictly wholesale. . . . They sold their imported goods in the original packages; they dealt only in large quantities, and left the retail business entirely in the hands of the Sierra Leone traders. . . . All this is now changed. The middleman's occupation is no longer what it used to be, as the great firms of importers have gradually become their own middlemen, and, while continuing to be wholesale merchants, they have developed retail business on their own account.[14]

Business, for the African middle class, became a risky and uncertain line of occupation, and white collar callings rose in estimation because of the security they gave. Thus, in the period between the two World Wars, the professions, in the narrow sense of law and medicine, and clerkships in the Government Civil Service, were the jobs to which most aspired. Indeed, until as late as 1946, as Dr Kenneth Little has affirmed, law and medicine still attracted the majority of a random sample of schoolboys interviewed.[15]

However, there are signs of incipient changes in the occupational rating. One of the questions in the Questionnaire to which reference has already been made concerned students' evaluations of a number of occupations.[16] The answers to this showed that while medicine is still highly rated, only thirteen per cent. gave it first place while thirty-five per cent. ranked it second among the occupations listed. On the other hand twenty-nine per cent. gave the highest rank to Puisne Judge while only one per cent. gave a similar position to a lawyer, which could mean a more discriminating evaluation of the profession these days, reserving the higher honours to those whose elevation to the Bench can be regarded as evidence of success at the Bar. Another interesting change is that the University lecturer was rated as of

[14] T. J. Alldridge, *A Transformed Colony* (London, Seeley and Co., 1910), pp. 73–5.

[15] K. L. Little, 'Structural Change in the Sierra Leone Protectorate', *Africa*, vol. xxv, No. 3 (July 1955), pp. 217–33.

[16] Cf. p. 91 *supra*.

highest prestige ranking by twenty-five per cent. of the students and of second place in the list of ten occupations by nineteen per cent. of the same respondents. The occupations and listing for highest rank were as follows:

	No.	%
Puisne Judge	26	29
Newspaper Editor	–	–
Medical Practitioner	12	13
Independent Businessman	11	12
Administrative Officer	4	4
University Lecturer	22	25
Member of House of Representatives	7	8
Lawyer	1	1
Minister of Religion	2	2
Civil Engineer	4	4

To the further question, 'suppose someone asked your advice on what would be the best occupation to aim toward in present day Sierra Leone, which occupation would you advise', the weighting was in favour of occupations concerned with farming and agriculture, education and business-commerce rather than with the professions as such.

Another feature of the changing social structure of Freetown is that occupational demarcations no longer correspond closely with ethnic distinctions. Indeed, it would be difficult now, except in the very broadest way, to categorize occupations in terms of ethnicity. In almost every occupation there are now to be found both Creoles and others of tribal origin, and the gap is narrowing. Personal achievement and technical capability are increasingly becoming the dominant criteria in job selection.

Further, general economic development has meant a change in the opportunity-structure of the society, which, in turn, has affected the chances for social mobility. More jobs have been created by the opening up of the provinces and newer types of occupations are being provided to meet the demands of contemporary development. More specifically, in the traditional fields of law and medicine, more magistrates and more doctors are now required to fill the vacancies created by the establishment of more courts and new hospitals.

The need for newer types of skill has also led to the creation of new appointments and the upgrading of certain other positions. For example, in the civil service, there are now appointments for a Town Planner, a Government Artist, and a Government Librarian–appointments which never existed twenty years ago. In addition, jobs which require technical rather than integrative skills have been upgraded in the past few years. For example, the post of Divisional Engineer in the Public Works Department now carries a salary comparable to that offered to medical practitioners in the Service.

The greatest factor that has influenced the opportunity structure, however, is the mining industry. The mining of diamond and iron ore especially, has meant new jobs and opportunities for many of the working class. Lunsar, the location of the iron ore industry which was a small hamlet of about twenty houses in 1929, now boasts a population of about 15,000. More important, the rich diamond deposits were found to be scattered throughout the provinces, and by 1950 it was impossible to safeguard the exclusive monopoly for diamond digging which had been granted to the Sierra Leone Selection Trust in 1931; and so in 1955 a new arrangement was made with the Company by which they gave up the exclusive monopoly for a compensation of a million and a half pounds and rights to a smaller area. The 'illicit' diamond diggings, while it robbed the Treasury of much-needed funds, did create wealth for many people in the provinces which placed them in an advantageous position to contest power with the Creoles of the peninsula area which did not command this source of wealth. The development of the communication system by the construction of roads has also meant more work employment for many. These and similar developments have in turn caused a rise in spending power and in employment in the distributive industries.

The changes affect the processes of social mobility by expanding the number of available social class positions in different parts of the stratification system. In terms of the *shape* of the stratification system, it can be said that, while in the nineteenth century, the stratification system was one in which a few families composed the class of élites with the majority of the population at the bottom of the ladder, today, the *shape* is more one that bulges in the middle, that is to say, the increase seems to be more in the expansion of the middle class.

Because of a number of factors, the old Creole aristocracy of the nineteenth century has suffered a reduction. With the decline in trade and the loss of the independent living which that had meant, appointments in the Colonial Service became the goal of the many. Secondly, the decision to make Hill Station a reservation for the Europeans meant that the Freetown community lost the easy atmosphere of cordiality which contiguity had implied between Europeans and their African colleagues. In addition, the Hut Tax War[17] and its consequences had sown seeds of mutual distrust between the Administration and the leaders of Creole society, as well as between the Creoles and the tribes.

This distrust was manifested in a number of overt ways. For example, an English judge staying at Government House in 1898 seems never to have dined with an African, nor had any social contacts with Sir Samuel Lewis or any other member of the Freetown Bar.[18] Again, in 1902, when the West African Medical Service was created, Freetown doctors who had rendered service in the past as colonial surgeons on an equality with their European colleagues, were relegated to a lower category as 'native' doctors, an inferior status from which merit could not promote them.

While the opportunities for Creole advancement were thus being reduced or confined, certain significant changes were occurring in other parts of the body politic. Educational opportunities, as we have noted, were being extended, thereby giving more people a chance to acquire and hold more remunerative occupations and so enhance their social class position. Socio-economic expansion has meant, in addition, an increase in the proportion of professional, business and clerical positions.

A further evidence of the occupational changes is the higher ranking of the political rôles. In the transition from a colonial dependency to a self-governing independent state, it is to the politician that all look for the necessary guidance and pronouncements. As will be developed in the following chapter, while the political rôle was honorary and amateur in the nineteenth century, today it is a highly remunerative and full-time employment.

[17] *Supra*, pp. 60–3. [18] Information communicated by Mr C. H. Fyfe.

Chapter 11

PROCESSES OF SOCIAL MOBILITY–POLITICAL POWER

In the past, most studies of political development have concentrated on an analysis of the formal organs of power. The Institute of Commonwealth Studies at Oxford in co-operation with Nuffield College, for example, has produced a series of volumes on the development of legislative councils in different parts of the British Empire. In these studies the legislature is treated mainly as a point of contact between the colonial aspirations of the area and imperial control, and examination is made of the relationships between different elements in the constitution. Concentration is on institutional development rather than on the individuals who participate in the institutions. Where individuals are mentioned, however, the emphasis is on formal prescribed behaviour and little attempt is made to analyse the social and psychological characteristics of the individuals who interact within the institutional context.[1] Yet it cannot be denied that some analysis of the society of which a political institution is a part must be essayed if a full and exhaustive understanding of the political process is expected.

One way we can approach this larger question is by looking at the individuals who played a part in the process. It is now generally recognized that the rôles and positions of individuals in the social structure of a society will affect the development of the character structure of such individuals, and that this in turn will influence the formation of their ideals and values and the manner and degree of their participation in the political decision-making process.[2]

The reasons for this are not far to seek. In the first place, political leaders, like all others, are human. They carry with them into the political arena their own set of individual interests,

[1] Cf. Martin Wight, *The Development of the Legislative Council* (London: Faber and Faber, 1947).

[2] E. Fromm, *Escape from Freedom* (New York: Rinehart, 1941), pp. 227ff.

prejudices and assumptions. We know from the researches of psychologists and sociologists that men's behaviour and decisions are influenced largely by their personal life experiences as well as the normative patterns of the society.

Further, changes in the social background of decision-makers can be a useful indication of overall social and economic changes in a society. In the history of Britain, for example, the noticeable change in the subject matter of debates from an almost exclusive preoccupation with matters of foreign policy and the constitution in the period before the First and Second Reform Bills to an increasing proportion of debates on matters of health and education could not have occurred but for the wider electorate and the new men who were entering Parliament after 1832 and 1867.

Power, according to Max Weber, consists in the probability that one of the parties in a social relationship will be able to carry out his will despite the opposing will of the other party to the relationship.[3] This must not be confused with authority. To say, for example, that a person has political authority is to say that the political formula assigns him power and that those who adhere to that formula expect him to have power and regard his exercise of it as just and proper. This further implies that a person may have or exercise power without the legitimate authority; in other words, though authority is always legitimate, power can either be legitimate or illegitimate.[4] Thus, in the West African political context, it was possible in the pre-independence period to have a situation in which authority and legitimate power were in the hands of the District Commissioner and his council, while a large amount of extra-legal influence or traditional power may have resided with the secret societies.

It is, however, extremely difficult to estimate the relative amounts of powerful influence in a given society because of the varied and kaleidoscopic forms and shapes power might take. Further, there is no calculus of influence to measure and compare the influence structures in one or more given societies.

[3] Max Weber, *The Theory of Social and Economic Organization*, trans. by A. M. Henderson and Talcott Parsons (New York: Oxford University Press, 1947), pp. 152ff.

[4] It seems to the writer untenable to regard all forms of power as illegitimate influence as Barber does. Cf. Barber, op. cit., p. 236.

In this chapter, we shall consider only the authority structure in the political sense. Of course, even in this limited sense, actual power was until recently in the hands of the British Administration. Although colonial rule, as the ex-Governor Anton Bertram pointed out, is in the final analysis the dictatorship of the Governor, yet it had been the practice from quite early in the history of the Colony to attempt to associate the inhabitants with the process of administration.[5] For example, the Sierra Leone Council of 1811 provided for a membership of the Chief Justice, the Colonial Secretary and 'one unofficial member from among the most considerable of the Protestant inhabitants'. However, the theory of a legislative council was still that of a homogeneous advisory body ready to support and back the Administration.

Thus, in analysing the criterion of political power, we shall be considering those who participated in the decision-making process regardless of the degree of actual power that they possessed. To the Africans, the nominated members in the legislature were conceived as having some degree of power.

In colonial areas, one can distinguish three classes which fit these conditions. These are the leaders in traditional societies, the European or alien rulers and the western educated Africans whose status is rooted in the urban conditions prevalent in the coastal towns. All three groups have supplied those who have wielded or still wield political power.

While the European group has tended to remain on the whole stable (for obvious reasons), the changes in the personnel, ideology and skills of the other two groups are marked, and it is suggested that these changes are crucial for an understanding of the political development of the respective countries. It is proposed, in this chapter, to examine the process of recruitment to the political élite, the movement of people in and out of positions of pre-eminence which Pareto called the 'circulation of élites', in the political development of Sierra Leone under British rule.

The most completely autonomous form of government which

[5] Anton Bertram, *The Colonial Service* (Cambridge: Cambridge University Press, 1930).
'These Councils, as far as the influence they have are dead letters and legislation is in the hands of the Governor.' Mary Kingsley, *West African Studies* (London, 1901), p. 259.

Sierra Leone ever had before independence was the first one, the government of the Black Poor who arrived from England in 1787. Granville Sharp was anxious that the settlement should be truly self-governing and should owe no obedience to any superior government. He therefore left it largely to the Settlers to suggest their own laws and elect their own officials. Quarrels, however, broke out and this first attempt at independence ended in failure when the struggling settlement was attacked by the Temnes and broken up.

When the settlement was refounded in 1791 by the newly formed Sierra Leone Company, it was administered by a council of eight persons, afterwards reduced to a Governor and two persons responsible to the Company Directors in London. This set-up of a Governor and Council, became the pattern for all future constitutions. It was continued in 1808 when Freetown became a crown colony, except that the Governor was now appointed by the Sovereign, and the laws had to be in keeping with English law and not repugnant to the British system.

It was the practice from quite early in the history of the Colony, as has been pointed out, for the Government to associate the inhabitants with the process of administration. Indeed there was almost complete local autonomy under hundredors and tithingmen until the Nova Scotian Rebellion in 1800. Further, Kenneth Macaulay, the trader, was appointed to the Council in 1815. This was in part evidence of the continued influence of the mercantile interest in the affairs of the Colony; and from that time it has been usual for the business interest to be represented in the legislature.

This advisory council of officials and nominated members lasted with but minor changes until 1863. During that period the population had grown from about two to forty thousand largely because of the addition of the Liberated Africans. Economically and socially also, the Colony had progressed. One of the effects of this socio-economic progress was a greater articulation of the political consciousness of the people. One of the earliest attempts at political organization was through the Mercantile Association founded in the mid-1850s and composed of the successful traders among both the Europeans and the Africans.

Thus by the 1860s the people were clearly ready for a change, and this was partially met in 1863 when the recommendations of Governor Blackall for a new constitution were approved. This resulted in a new charter which divided the Governor's Council into two–an Executive and a Legislative Council. The first two unofficial members into the Legislative Council were Charles Heddle, the prosperous ground-nut trader, who had served in the former council, and John Ezzidio, an African merchant who was appointed on the recommendation of the Mercantile Association.[6]

Ezzidio's appointment set a pattern in two ways. Though Blackall might have hoped that the Mercantile Association would have returned a European, yet the precedent set in this case of appointing an African was respected, and subsequent Governors chose Africans to serve as unofficial members after Ezzidio. Thus, representation took on an added significance for the people, since it was now an African or indigenous representation. Secondly, succeeding Governors chose men from the same class of successful merchants–men whose position in the society had been validated in terms of wealth and of social status.

Thus, Governor Kennedy appointed William Grant in 1869 and Henry Lumpkin and Syble Boyle in 1870. Governor Rowe appointed the successful Liberated African contractor and merchant, Isaac Benjamin Pratt, in 1879, and T. J. Sawyerr, the wealthy bookseller, on his second term of office, in 1883. In 1893, Governor Fleming chose Daniel Jarrett, businessman and trader. And even Cardew, during whose administration Creole influence was limited, chose Theophilus Colenso Bishop, grocer and hardware merchant of Water and Rawdon Streets, in 1894. Other successful merchants for whom seats were found in the legislature included J. J. Thomas (made a C.M.G. in 1908) and John Malamah Thomas, whose house, decorated with carved heads, still stands and is still owned by the family in Little East Street, in an area where most Creoles have sold out their ancestral properties to Lebanese and other traders.[7] In terms of any meaningful criterion these men belonged to the group of western educated Africans. They were uninfluenced in any crucial sense by tribal mores while conforming in cultural details to

[6] *Supra* p. 56.
[7] C. H. Fyfe, *A History of Sierra Leone*, op. cit., passim.

behaviour governed by western standards. They were city fathers, officers in their various church organizations and owners of town properties. To wealth and status was now added the distinction of advising and deliberating with the law-makers of the society. During this period of successful commerce, many traders sent their children to England to study for one or other of the learned professions.

With the choice of one of these returned scholars, the barrister Sir Samuel Lewis, as a council member, we pass from the period of the merchant to the period of the professionals. This fact, that the nominated unofficials after 1882 were drawn increasingly from the professional ranks rather than from the mercantile or business interest points to the changes in the prestige order and economic basis of the society. Both groups, however, belonged to the social élite, the difference being that there had occurred a shift in the kind of occupation of highest ranking.

During this period–from 1882 to the promulgation of a new constitution in 1924–the nominated members included such Creoles as Claude E. Wright, Abraham Spencer Hebron, A. J. Shorunkeh Sawyerr–all barristers; E. H. Cummings who had gone into the trading business of his father, and Claudius May, then proprietor of *The Weekly News*.

Despite this quasi-representative element in the Council, it was not intended that it should be a debating chamber or that the African was there to represent what can be called the national interest. The function of the unofficial nominated member had been described by the Duke of Buckingham in his Circular Despatch of 1868 as follows:

> You will naturally understand that holding his seat by nomination of the Crown, he has been selected for it in the expectation and in the confidence that he will co-operate with the Crown on any important question without strong and substantial reason.[8]

Between 1865, when a Select Committee of the House of Commons recommended that the British Government should assume no further responsibility in West Africa, and 1896, the year of the declaration of the Protectorate, British interests had

[8] Martin Wight, *The Development of the Legislative Council*, op. cit., p. 112.

extended into the interior of the settlement and the area had come to be regarded as a British sphere of influence. In 1893 J. C. Parkes, who was superintendent of the Department of Native Affairs described the situation in a notable memorandum to the Colonial Secretary for transmission to London as one 'in which we exercise all the authority incidental to a protectorate without venturing to declare that it is one'.[9] He suggested that a protectorate ought to be declared over the area of influence and that instead of the 'large armed force in almost every corner of the sphere of influence' there should be Political Agents established at various parts and that these Agents should be Africans, which for Parkes would have meant Creoles. But Hamilton of the Colonial Office objected to any such use of African Agents on the excuse that they were not forthcoming. He wrote:

> But Mr Parkes is an exception and I don't for a moment suppose we could get half-a-dozen natives like him who could be trusted for this kind of work.[10]

Hemming was even more emphatic when he minuted:

> We could not depend on them and they would be likely to get us into all sorts of difficulties. I should much prefer a couple of good European travelling Commanders who should go about the country and hear complaints and settle difficulties, taking with them an escort of Police.[11]

In 1896 a Protectorate was duly declared over the hinterland of Sierra Leone. Two years after occurred the Hut Tax Insurrection and the embittering of relationship between Colony and Protectorate which was one of its sorry consequences. Notwithstanding the report of David Chalmers who was sent out to investigate the situation, Joseph Chamberlain, the Secretary of State for the Colonies, decided to support the view expressed by Governor Cardew that too much political power should not be granted to the people of the Colony especially with the added responsibility for the Protectorate which the Government had assumed.[12]

[9] C.O. 267/400. [10] C.O. 267/406. [11] C.O. 267/407.
[12] J. D. Hargreaves, 'Establishment of the Sierra Leone Protectorate', *Cambridge Historical Journal*, vol. XII (1956).

Thus unofficial representation in the Legislative Council remained substantially the same notwithstanding the enlargement of the territory of the country.

By the end of the First World War, there was growing dissatisfaction with the constitution and with the rate of political progress in British West Africa in general. The National Congress of British West Africa – a body made up predominantly of western educated Africans and formed in 1920 – was foremost in this quest for more representation.[13] In 1924, under Sir Ransford Slater, the Sierra Leone Constitution was revised to provide, as Slater put it, for the 'guarded introduction' of the elective principle by allowing for the election of three members to the Council – two for the urban areas and one for the rural area of the Colony. The elections were to be held on a restricted franchise of which literacy was one of the qualifications for the vote.

The introduction of the elective principle did not, however, affect the functions and powers of the new Council which did not differ very much from the old. Sierra Leone still remained a crown colony with a Legislative Council having an official majority.[14] Politically it would seem that the significance of the 1924 Constitution lay in the fact that quite apart from the increase in African representation and the introduction of the elective principle, it confirmed the unitary constitution which originated when the Order in Council of 28 August 1895, gave the Legislative Council power to legislate for Colony and Protectorate alike. A single legislature meant that the distinction between Colony and Protectorate had lost its constitutional meaning.

Under this 1924 Constitution, the elected members were drawn from the class of Creole social élites. The two urban members elected in 1924 were E. S. Beoku Betts and H. C. Bankole Bright, and their partnership lasted until 1937 when Beoku Betts resigned to take up appointment with the Government as Police Magistrate. The member representing the Rural

[13] Section 19 of the Constitution of the National Congress of British West Africa reads:

'The aims of the Congress shall be to aid in the development of the political institutions of British West Africa under the Union Jack, so as eventually to take her place beside the sister nations of the Empire, and in time, to ensure within her borders the government of the people, by the people, for the people.'

[14] Sierra Leone Legislative Council Order in Council 1924.

Area was A. E. Tuboku-Metzger. Both Sir Ernest Beoku Betts and Dr Herbert Bankole Bright's fathers had been successful traders and businessmen, and they had been sent to England to qualify in the learned professions. Mr Tuboku-Metzger, after graduating as the first Fourah Bay College student to receive a first class honours qualification in the Licentiate in Theology of Durham University under the terms of the affiliation, went into the Government Civil Service where he rose to a position of great responsibility. They were all men of means who could afford the luxury of politics as a sideline or hobby. In 1929 Mr J. G. Hyde, another barrister, succeeded Mr Tuboku-Metzger as the rural member. In the by-election of 1937, Mr T. E. Nelson-Williams, another barrister, replaced Sir Justice Beoku Betts. On the whole, personalities rather than issues dominated these early election campaigns.[15]

Political representation throughout the life of the 1924 Constitution was drawn overwhelmingly from this class of social élites. Lawyers like Otto During and Hotobah During, doctors like George Reffell, successful businessmen and real estate owners like J. C. O. Crowther, dominated the political scene.

The 1924 Constitution had also provided for seven nominated members of whom three must be Paramount Chiefs of the Protectorate.[16] Thus, in extending African representation to the Protectorate cognizance was given to those whose positions in the society had already been validated by other criteria. Chiefs were, by any standard, at the top of the societal pyramid of their respective sub-cultures, and were now drawn into the central legislature with the socially privileged of the Colony to deliberate together with the imperial power in the exciting process of law-making.

It is not surprising, therefore, considering the social background of the total African representation, that the orientation of the Council was cautious and conservative. The new men of political power were men of status and of wealth in their several societies. Both the traditional social élite and the westernized social élite expected in due course to fall heirs to

[15] T. N. Goddard, *Handbook of Sierra Leone* (London, Grant Richards, 1925), pp. 97ff.

[16] Cf. *Sierra Leone Daily Mail*, 30 October 1937.

this political structure of which they were now a part on the eventual withdrawal of the British government. Their built-in conservatism, however, militated against any pressure for radical changes or for a hurried acceleration of political development.

This leisurely cavalier attitude towards government and politics began to be seriously challenged in 1938 with the foundation of the West African Youth League by Mr I. T. A. Wallace Johnson, a journalist who had studied at the People's University in Moscow. Unlike the Sierra Leone National Congress, it was not composed exclusively of the westernized social élite. Its standpoint was socialist and anti-colonial and it regarded itself as the mouthpiece of the 'toiling masses'. It published a newspaper, *The African Standard*, through which it agitated for greater African representation in the political order and the eventual withdrawal of the European element. It did not confine itself to sedate constitutional language, but employed the tone of the radical and the revolutionary and used techniques of ridicule, caricature and lampoon to attack the government and personnel of the day and to undermine the accustomed respectability they had engendered in the people. Of this movement, Professor Macmillan commented thus:

> It is a new phenomenon that Freetown for a year or more has been greatly stirred by the activities of a so-called Youth League. Night after night the Wilberforce Hall has been crowded to the doors and windows by those assembled to consider and foment grievances, and though the subjects of protests and demonstrations have by no means always been well chosen or well founded, the ventilation of constitutional or labour grievances has begun to bridge the old deep cleavage between the Creoles and the peoples of the Protectorate. Creole leaders, in short, not uninfluenced by the 'ideologies' of the new age, are coming into their own as the natural leaders of discontent wherever it may happen to show itself.[17]

Because of its marxist, militant and anti-colonial orientation, the Government found a reason during the war years to keep in confinement with prisoners of war its organizing Secretary, Mr I. T. A. Wallace Johnson.

[17] Meek, Macmillan and Hussey, op. cit., p. 76.

Other protest and openly individualistic movements aimed at increasing African participation, but none achieved such a degree of popular approval or sensational interest as the Youth League; and while the League genuinely tried to serve both Creoles and tribal inhabitants, the newer movements originated as predominantly Colony or Protectorate pressure groups. The only unifying attempt with any degree of popular support was the *People's Party* founded in 1949 by a Creole politician and clergyman, Rev. E. N. Jones who, as a conscious attempt to meet the tribal inhabitants, had taken the name Laminah Sankoh. The more parochially rooted were the *National Council* formed in August 1950 under the leadership of Dr Bankole Bright which was frankly committed to safeguard Creole and Colony interests; the *Sierra Leone Organization Society* (S.O.S.), founded in 1946 by a group of young western trained intellectuals from the Protectorate, was anti-Colony in its orientation and at the same time anti-traditional.[18] As F. S. Anthony, one of its foundation members, wrote in the *Sierra Leone Weekly News* for 18 October 1947:

> The District Councils and the Protectorate Assembly are merely composed of the natural rulers and therefore are not democratic institutions from which an electoral body can be formed for the peoples of the Protectorate.[19]

In 1950 the S.O.S. and the *Peoples Party* amalgamated to form the *Sierra Leone Peoples Party* under the leadership of Dr (now Sir) Milton Margai.

In 1951 a new constitution was introduced which provided for an elected unofficial African majority and party rule. After the election the Sierra Leone Peoples Party emerged as the

[18] In a memorandum to the Government on the 1947 Constitutional Proposals, the S.O.S. wrote as follows: 'During the twenty-five years of the existence of the present Legislative Council constitution, Government has never nominated the "Progressive and younger elements" outside the Chief's class to sit in the Legislative Council. . . . It is . . . necessary that definite provisions should be made for the inclusion of the new progressive and literate element into the membership of the new Legislative Council.'

[19] F. S. Anthony, 'Memorandum of the S.O.S.', *Sierra Leone Weekly News*, 18 October 1947, p. 3.

For further information on these post-war movements, cf. the writings of Dr M. L. Kilson in *West Africa*. I am indebted to Dr Kilson for drawing my attention to the printed and typed materials of these parties. Also cf. D. J. R. Scott, *Five Elections in Africa*, ed. Mackenzie and Robinson (Oxford: Clarendon Press, 1960), pp. 187ff.

majority party and was duly invited to form the government.[20]

Thus, wrote Dr Scott:

> The country was committed to party politics. The National Council, the majority party in the limited field of declared party contest, was particularly aggrieved, and the militantly anti-Creole, or at least Protectorate-first, views expressed by the S.L.P.P. leader in the Protectorate Assembly during the preceding year left a large part of Creoledom resentful and suspicious.[21]

An analysis of the African membership of this Council underscores some of the economic and social changes which were occurring in Sierra Leone during the period as well as the voting habits of the now wider electorate. Of the twenty-two African unofficial members, eight were Paramount Chiefs, two were medical doctors, two barristers, one a university lecturer, two businessmen, two retired civil servants, one ex-trade union official, one minister of religion, one retired baker, and one ex-Native Tribal Authority employee. Thus, while the social élite class, traditional as well as western urbanized, was still significantly represented, there had emerged representation from individuals who do not reflect the same degree of correlation between class, status and political power. These new men derive their claims, not from any descent or wealth, but from their specialized skills and talents or as leaders in their ethnic or religious communities. They belong to the group of rising literate Africans who are now, throughout the continent, challenging the political monopoly which had been enjoyed by the western oriented social élite. They hope to oust the older groups not only as wielders of political power but also as a standard-setting group in the social sphere.

The question here arises as to whether this lack of correlation

[20] The question whether party rule was envisaged in 1951 has sometimes been debated. But as Sir Milton Margai said in the House: 'It was simply natural that whatever doubt he had when he found that the group I was dealing with–call it a party, a small community or merely a number of people–was in a majority that he decided that I had to be consulted in selecting Executive Council. This does not mean that I picked the people; he suggested names and I approved or disapproved of them.' Cf. *Legislative Council Debates, Session 1951–52*, vol. 1, p. 271 (Proceedings of 31 January 1952); Also vol. 1, p. 89 (Proceedings of 28 November 1951).

[21] D. J. R. Scott, op. cit., p. 191.

can be regarded as evidence of the democratization of the society. Political sociologists have drawn attention to this process in other societies where as they become democratic, members of non-privileged groups have acquired a share of political influence at least more nearly equal in amount to that of the members of the upper classes. Indeed, one writer goes so far as to say with reference to the United States of America that 'the political weight of a class is in inverse relation to its average wealth'.[22]

The revision of the constitution in 1956, replacing the old Legislative Council by a House of Representatives and dropping the literacy requirement in the franchise for all voters except for certain categories of women in the provinces, continued the process already begun in 1951.[23] The new House provided for a Speaker, four ex-officio members, two nominated members, fourteen directly elected members from the Colony and twenty-five from the Protectorate together with one Paramount Chief from each provincial administrative district.

The requirement that all members of the House of Representatives should be literate in English limited the field from which candidates could be selected; yet there were, among the candidates in the 1957 election, thirty small businessmen, five ministers of religion, two junior clerks of District Councils, a health inspector, an agricultural supervisor and two supervising teachers.[24] On the other hand, a factor which contributed to the broadening of the social basis of political representation was the payment made to members–a principle which was established in 1951. As Dr Scott has written on the 1957 Elections:

> Candidates in the Protectorate, the Colony rural area, and Sherbro mostly admitted frankly to an interest in the material rewards to be derived from membership of the House and the possibility of office. It could hardly have been otherwise; they were largely retired persons or farmers or traders in a very small way of business and observation of the previous legislature suggested that it was possible to do reasonably well in politics, besides acquiring the style Honourable. . . . In Freetown there was naturally greater sophistication in

[22] C. Arnold Anderson, 'The Need for a Functional Theory of Social Class', *Rural Sociology*, vol. XIX (1954), p. 152.

[23] Sierra Leone (House of Representatives) Order in Council 1956.

[24] W. J. Mackenzie & K. Robinson (eds.), op. cit., p. 229.

speech and probably in thought. In the middle-class English world of the Creole it had long been desirable to gain this sort of prestige even at the cost of personal inconvenience, and the possibility that honourable office might in some intangible way further a professional career was familiar.[25]

Thus it had become possible for various sections of the society to compete more equally for political influence.

In March 1960 all the different political parties represented in the House of Representatives decided at the Round-Table Talks preparatory to the Constitutional Conference held in London in June of that year to form a United National Front in order 'to bring the resources of all parties, sections and organizations to bear on the immediate problems which will be discussed at the Constitutional Conference . . . and other problems thereafter . . . including the implementation of Independence and the efficient administration of Government'.[26]

One of the results of this United Front was the formation of a coalition government after the London constitutional talks. Thus the Sierra Leone Peoples Party with its uncontested Protectorate support was able to share its powers and responsibilities of government with the other political parties, and one of the more relevant consequences of this for our purpose is that there emerged once more Creoles participating at the ministerial level in the government of their country without first accepting the tribal orientation of the dominant political power. Thus the provincial leadership first challenged the Creoles in the political order and having wrested political initiative now felt themselves strong and secure enough to share this power with the old leadership.

Another significant factor is the increasing participation in the decision-making process of occupations unknown in the nineteenth century political arena. The baker, the accountant, the trade unionist, the teacher–men whose occupations depend, not on traditional cultures, but on the twin processes of industrialization and westernization–can now rise to power with the help of western organized political parties.

Another significant change, corollary to this, is that voters no

[25] W. J. Mackenzie & K. Robinson (eds.), op. cit., p. 265.
[26] *Sierra Leone Daily Mail*, 26 March 1960, p. 1.

longer return only those whose status has been already validated. Like voters in England after the Reform Bill of 1832, the first reaction in 1924 was to return the old class of amateur politicians of wealth and social status. After 1951 the picture changes: the rising career politician, without traditional support or professional prestige, is able to make use of local advantages to win elections. A further question which this poses is whether this disconsensus between wealth, status and power is an index of greater individuation of the society or whether it is an index of political and social instability which is temporary and that future development will be towards greater crystallization of all three criteria in the hands of the same persons.

How far the social background of these new men of power will influence political debates and decisions is a matter for further study. In England, it will be recalled, there was greater emphasis on questions of social welfare and justice after the Second Reform Bill due largely to the wider electorate and the more broadly based House of Commons. In time, of course, these new men of power will be able to translate their influences into social advantages for their children that will help the latter to achieve higher ranking status positions. A crucial question is whether they will, when they reach social élite position, accept the present all-embracing process of westernization as their prestige standard or whether they will create new patterns for others to follow. In short, whether in the political order, the new Sierra Leone personality at the termination of British rule will reflect traditional mores and structure or whether it will show the effect of imperatives operating in western social structures.

Conclusion

Chapter 12

SOCIAL CHANGE AND THE FUTURE OF THE SOCIAL STRATIFICATION SYSTEM

THIS study has concerned the stratification system in Creole society. It must be emphasized again that a class system is only part of an interdependent whole, that as a society is a continuum and not static, so too is its class or status system. Thus it is not surprising that the class structure changes in response to changes in other parts of the society.

The question which the study poses is whether it has any theoretical relevance or whether it has any comparative usefulness for studying conditions of social change in other emergent territories. Firstly, it would be difficult, almost impossible, to produce a cogent theory that can account for social change even in this limited field. Too little is known about the history of class structures and about the way they respond to social changes to provide any meaningful theory.

Nevertheless there seems to emerge a pattern of change which may have some theoretical meaning and could form a basis or yard stick of comparison with similar societies.

Freetown society we have seen has passed from a particularistic to a universalistic-oriented form of society. At the beginning of the British colonial rule, the pattern was such that all the crucial criteria which make up class position, especially the economic, status and political dimensions of class, were concentrated in the hands of a few, the Settlers. The period between about 1830 and 1870 saw a disconsensus between these three criteria and the process of fusion between Settlers and Liberated Africans to form the Creoles. These Creoles constituted an élite group (excluding the European administration) in which were conserved the high-ranking positions in the economic, social and political orders until they began to be seriously challenged by the indigenous inhabitants especially after 1945.

This challenge, accompanied by rapid economic and political changes in the society, has meant a new and recurrent disparity between the three dimensions.

The crystallization of the first period was based largely on status and the favourable treatment of the Government. The crystallization of variables in the second period was based on economic wealth made in trade and translated very substantially into land holdings.

But this kind of élitism, this kind of land holding aristocratic élite, has disappeared. Development and industrialization, however minor, are creating newer job opportunities and a newer basis for wealth, for status and for political power. In place of land which is limited and thereby more amenable to monopoly practices, industrialization brings a money economy instead of subsistence, and the means whereby wealth can be created in many more ways than wealth based on land would reasonably allow.

Another factor which is making for change is the corresponding development of urbanization. More and more people are moving from rural to urban conditions, either to the areas of intense economic activity where technology is rapidly bringing urbanism like the mines, or to the new urban centres growing up as administrative or political units. Thus an increasing number are removed from the restraints and controls of rural social codes and are flung into the whirlpool and anonymity of the city where different values prevail and different traditions are established.

An outstanding effect of this is the emergence of a new middle class. These are on the one hand the young and the malcontents of the old aristocratic order and on the other, the young and western educated members of the old tribal groups who at the same time are unconnected with the tribal social élite. Many of these see their future through the political order and through nationalism. For all groups involved in the social changes created by industrialization and its twin process, urbanization, this new middle class has the most to lose and the most to gain. To lose means to return to a society in which they could not function effectively; to win, means to gain new status and a large share in the power mechanisms and institutions of society.

Many were also able to benefit materially from the economic

structure even though they had no status or political success. Consequently there developed a greater separation of social class components. Thus we have today the division to which attention has already been drawn in the text.

But if one were to attempt to answer here the question posed in the last chapter, viz. whether the present disconsensus is an index of greater societal individuation or whether it is an index of a temporary situation, the answer seems to be the latter rather more so than the former. If the kind of process C. Wright Mills has described in *The Power Elite* has any relevance for our study it is that there will come a time in the development of industrialization when the separate dimensions of class will converge again in the hands of an élite, as Mills has argued that political power, military power and economic power are tending to concentrate in a small élite in the United States.

The economic and political components converge because, it is argued, they become functionally interdependent. The men of political power will come more and more to depend on men of economic power to attain their position. Election campaigns, for example, will become increasingly expensive. And on the other hand the men of economic power will depend on the men of political power for the right atmosphere in terms of governmental regulation and supervision for the prosecution of their trade or business. It is further argued that the elements of status and prestige also tend to be lodged in those of economic and political power. And these will validate each other, and so by processes of selective mating, prolong inculcation of certain patterns and preferences, a new élite in whom the crucial class dimensions are concentrated, will emerge. And the development of the class system will have moved another full circle from crystallization to disconsensus, to crystallization to disconsensus and again to crystallization. If Sierra Leone remains a geographical and political unit, the process would have engulfed all its citizens and would depend on some other trend to upset the pattern.

The present crystallization in the American scene, it has been suggested, is due largely to the decreasing immigration from outside. A similar process will occur in Freetown when all its inhabitants have been brought into the one social system.

All this does not mean that a firm prediction of the future of the class structure in Sierra Leone can be made. But the conclusions stated here are tempting; at any rate an understanding of the trends and imperatives operating in our society and the future outlines that are being formed is necessary by all those interested in the well-being of our country.

Appendix

HANDBILL RECRUITING THE BLACK POOR

IT having been maturely and humanely considered, by what means a support might be given to the Blacks, who seek the protection of this government; it is found that no place is so fit and proper, as the Grain Coast of Africa; where the necessaries of life may be supported by the force of industry and moderate labour, and life rendered very comfortable. It has been meditated to send Blacks to Nova Scotia, but this plan is laid aside, as that country is unfit and improper for the said Blacks.

The Committee for the Black Poor, accordingly recommended Henry Smeathman, Esq.,[1] who is acquainted with this part of the coast of Africa, to take charge of all the said persons, who are desirous of going with him; and to give them all fit and proper encouragement, agreeable with the humanity of the British Government.

Bateson's Coffee House, 17 May 1786.

By desire of the Committee
JONAS HANWAY, Chairman.

Those who are desirous of profiting by this opportunity, of settling in one of the most pleasant and fertile countries in the known world, may apply for further information to Mr SMEATHMAN, the Author of the Plan, and Agent for the Settlement, at the Office for Free Africans, No. 14 Cannon Street.

[1] Cf. Granville Sharp, *Short Sketch of Temporary Regulations* for the Intended Settlement (dated 3 July 1786), p. 41; *The Gentlemen's Magazine*, 1786, vol. LIV, p. 620.

SELECTED BIBLIOGRAPHY

Source Material of Theoretical Relevance:

BOOKS

Barber, B. *Social Stratification*. New York: Harcourt, Brace, 1957.

Bendix, R. *et al. Class, Status and Power*. Glencoe, Ill.: Free Press, 1953.

Cole, G. D. H. *Studies in Class Structure*. London: Kegan Paul, 1955.

Cuber, J. F. and Kenkel, W. F. *Social Stratification*. New York: Appleton-Century-Crofts, 1954.

Dollard, J. *Caste and Class in a Southern Town*. New York: Harper & Bros., 1949.

Durkheim, E. *The Elementary Forms of the Religious Life*. Translated by J. W. Swain, Glencoe, Ill.: Free Press, 1947.

Fromm, E., *Escape From Freedom*. New York: Rinehart, 1941.

Linton, R. *The Study of Man*. New York: Appleton-Century-Crofts, 1936.

MacIver, R. M. and Page, C. H. *Society*. New York: Rinehart, 1949.

Marshall, T. H. *Citizenship and Other Essays*. Cambridge: Cambridge University Press, 1950.

Morton, R. K. *Social Theory and Social Structure*. Revised edition. Glencoe, Ill.: Free Press, 1957.

Parsons, T. *Essays in Sociological Theory, Pure and Applied*. Revised edition. Glencoe, Ill.: Free Press, 1954.

Pope, L. *Millhands and Preachers*. New Haven: Yale University Press, 1942.

Reissman, L. *Class in American Society*. Glencoe, Ill.: Free Press, 1959.

Sorokin, P. A. *Social Mobility*. New York: Harper & Bros., 1927.

Tonnies, F. *Gemeinschaft und Gesellschaft*. Translated and edited by C. P. Loomis as *Fundamental Concepts of Sociology*. New York: American Book Co., 1940.

Veblen, T. *Theory of the Leisure Class*. New York: Macmillan, 1912.

Weber, H. *The Protestant Ethic and the Spirit of Capitalism*. Translated by Talcott Parsons. London: Allen & Unwin, 1930.

——, *From Max Weber: Essays in Sociology*. Translated by H. H. Gerth and C. W. Mills. New York: Oxford University Press, 1946.

——, *The Theory of Social and Economic Organisation*. Translated by A. M. Henderson and Talcott Parsons. New York: Oxford University Press, 1947.

Wight, M. *The Development of the Legislative Council.* London: Faber and Faber, 1947.

Williams, E. *Capitalism and Slavery.* Chapel Hill: University of Carolina Press, 1944.

Wilson, L. and Kolb, W. L. *Sociological Analysis.* New York: Harcourt, Brace, 1949.

ARTICLES and PERIODICALS

Anderson, C. A. 'The Need for a Functional Theory of Social Class', *Rural Sociology,* Vol. XIX (1954), pp. 152–60.

Davis, Kingsley. 'A Conceptual Analysis of Stratification', *American Sociological Review,* Vol. VII (June 1942), pp. 309–21.

Lenski, G. 'Status Crystallisation: A Non-vertical Dimension of Social Status', *American Sociological Review,* Vol. XIX (1954), pp. 405–13.

Tumin, M. M. 'Some Principles of Stratification: A Critical Analysis', *American Sociological Review,* Vol. XVIII (1953), pp. 387–94.

Source Material on the Freetown Data:

PUBLIC DOCUMENTS

Great Britain, Public Record Office, *Colonial Office, Despatches and Reports.* Series No. C.O. 267/.

Great Britain, Public Record Office, *Colonial Office, Sessional Papers and Council Minutes.* Series No. C.O. 270/.

Great Britain, Parliamentary Papers, Vol. VII (*Report of the Commissioners of Inquiry into the State of* Colony of Sierra Leone, 1827).

Great Britain, Parliamentary Papers, Vol. XXXVII (*Report of Colonel Ord, the Commissioner Appointed to Inquire Into the Condition of the British* Settlements on the West Coast of Africa, 1865).

Sierra Leone, *Census Reports* 1881–1931.

BOOKS

Alldridge, T. J. *A Transformed Colony.* London: Seeley, 1910.

Banton, M. *West African City.* London: Oxford University Press, 1957.

Blyden, E. *Christianity, Islam and the Negro Race.* 2nd Edition, London: 1889.

Clarke, R. *Sierra Leone Manners and Customs.* London: B. White, 1843.

Crooks, J. J. *History of the Colony of Sierra Leone*. Dublin: Simkin, 1903.

Dallas, R. C. *The History of the Maroons, from their Origin to the Establishment of their Chief Tribe at Sierra Leone, etc.* 2 Vols. London: Longman & Rees, 1803.

Falconbridge, A. M. *Two Voyages to Sierra Leone 1791–93*. London: 1794.

Fyfe, C. *A History of Sierra Leone*. Oxford: Oxford University Press, 1962.

Goddard, T. N. *The Handbook of Sierra Leone*. London: Grant Richards, 1925.

Groves, C. P. *The Planting of Christianity in Africa*. London: Lutterworth, 1948.

Hargreaves, J. D. *A Life of Sir Samuel Lewis*. London: Oxford University Press, 1958.

Hoare, P. *Memoirs of Granville Sharp*. London: Colburn, 1820.

Ingham, E. G. *Sierra Leone After A Hundred Years*. London: Seeley, 1894.

Kingsley, M. *West African Studies*. London: Macmillan, 1901.

Kuczynski, R. R. *A Demographic Survey of the British Colonial Empire*. 2 Vols. London: Oxford University Press, 1948.

Lewis, Roy. *Sierra Leone: A Modern Portrait*. London: H.M. Stationery Office, 1954.

Little, K. L. *The Mende of Sierra Leone*. London: Kegan Paul, 1951.

Luke, Sir H. *A Bibliography of Sierra Leone*. 2nd edition. London: Oxford University Press, 1925.

Mackenzie, W. J. and Robinson, K. E. *Five Elections in Africa*. Oxford: Clarendon Press, 1960.

Martin, E. C. *The British West African Settlements 1750–1821*. London: Oxford University Press, 1927.

Matthews, J. *A Voyage to the River Sierra Leone*. London: B. White, 1788.

Meek, C. K. *et al. Europe and West Africa*. London: Oxford University Press, 1940.

[Melville, E.]. *A Residence at Sierra Leone*. Edited by Hon. Mrs Norton. London: John Murray, 1849.

Poole, T. E. *Life, Scenery and Customs in Sierra Leone*. 2 Vols. London: Longman & Rees, 1850.

Seddall, F. *Missionary History of Sierra Leone*. London: Hartchard, 1874.

Shreeve, W. W. *Sierra Leone: The Principal British Colony on the West Coast*. London: B. White, 1847.

Thompson, F. W. Butt. *Sierra Leone in History and Tradition*. London: Witherby, 1926.

Thompson, T. J. *Jubilee and Centenary Volume of Fourah Bay College.* Freetown: Elsiemay, 1930.

Wadstrom, C. B. *An Essay on Colonization.* London: Hindmarsh, 1795.

ARTICLES and PERIODICALS

Archibald, A. 'Story of Deportation of Negroes from Nova Scotia to Sierra Leone', *Coll. of the Nova Scotian Historical Society*, Halifax, Vol. VII (1889–91), pp. 130–47.

Easmon, M. C. F. 'Sierra Leone Doctors', *Sierra Leone Studies*, N.S., No. 6 (June 1956).

Fyfe, C. H. 'European and Creole Influences in the Interior of Sierra Leone Before 1896', *Sierra Leone Studies*, N.S., No. 6 (June 1956), pp. 113–23.

——, 'The Life and Times of John Ezzidio', *Sierra Leone Studies*, N.S., No. 4 (June 1955), pp. 213–23.

——, 'The Sierra Leone Press in the Nineteenth Century', *Sierra Leone Studies*, N.S., No. 8 (June 1957), pp. 226–36.

Hargreaves, J. D. 'Establishment of the Sierra Leone Protectorate', *Cambridge Historical Journal*, Vol. XII (1956), pp. 56–80.

Jones-Quartey, K. A. B. 'Sierra Leone's Role in the Development of Ghana 1820–1930', *Sierra Leone Studies*, N.S., No. 10 (June 11, 1958), pp. 73–84.

Little, K. L. 'The Significance of the West African Creole for Africanist and Afro-American Studies', *Journal of African Affairs*, Vol. 49, No. 197 (December 1950), pp. 308–19.

——, 'Structural Change in the Sierra Leone Protectorate', *Africa*, Vol. XXV, No. 3 (July 1955), pp. 217–33.

Porter, A. T. 'Religious Affiliation in Freetown, Sierra Leone', *Africa*, Vol. XXIII, No. 1 (January 1953), pp. 3–14.

Smith, T. W. 'The Loyalists at Shelburne', *Coll. of the Nova Scotian Historical Society*, Halifax, Vol. V.

Turner, H. W. 'The Church of the Lord', *Journal of African History*, vol. III, 1962.

Wilson, H. S. 'The Changing Image of the Sierra Leone Colony in the Works of E. W. Blyden', *Sierra Leone Studies*, N.S., No. 11 (December 1958), pp. 136–48.

UNPUBLISHED MATERIAL

Cox-George, N. A. 'Financial System of a West African Colony in Relation to Economic Development.' Unpublished Ph.D. Thesis, London University, 1954.

Mellor, C. R. 'British Policy in Relation to Sierra Leone.' Unpublished M.A. Thesis, London University, 1935.

OTHER SOURCES

Church Missionary Records at C.M.S. House, Salisbury Square, London, England.

Clarkson, J. *Mission to America.* Manuscript in Public Archives of Nova Scotia, Halifax, N.S., Canada.

Sierra Leone Newspapers in the Nineteenth and Twentieth Centuries now housed at the British Museum Newspaper Library (Colindale) London, England.

INDEX

Printed by
Jarrold & Sons Ltd
Norwich, Norfolk